Meeting SEN
in the Curriculum:

RELIGIOUS EDUCATION

Other titles in the Meeting SEN in the Curriculum series:

Meeting Special Needs in English
Tim Hurst
1 84312 157 3

Meeting Special Needs in Maths
Brian Sharp
1 84312 158 1

Meeting Special Needs in Modern Foreign Languages
Sally McKeown
1 84312 165 4

Meeting Special Needs in Citizenship
Alan Combes
1 84312 169 7

Meeting Special Needs in History
Richard Harris and Ian Luff
1 84312 163 8

Meeting Special Needs in Design and Technology
Louise Davies
1 84312 166 2

Meeting Special Needs in Art
Kim Earle and Gill Curry
1 84312 161 1

Meeting Special Needs in Music
Victoria Jacquiss and Diane Paterson
1 84312 168 9

Meeting Special Needs in ICT
Mike North and Sally McKeown
1 84312 160 3

Meeting Special Needs in Science
Carol Holden
1 84312 159 X

Meeting Special Needs in Geography
Diane Swift
1 84312 162 X

Meeting Special Needs in PE and Sport
Crispin Andrews
1 84312 164 6

Meeting SEN
in the Curriculum:

RELIGIOUS

EDUCATION

Dilwyn Hunt

 David Fulton Publishers

David Fulton Publishers Ltd
The Chiswick Centre, 414 Chiswick High Road, London W4 5TF

www.fultonpublishers.co.uk

First published in Great Britain by David Fulton Publishers

10 9 8 7 6 5 4 3 2 1

David Fulton Publishers is a division of Granada Learning Limited, part of ITV plc.

Copyright © Dilwyn Hunt 2005

Note: The right of Dilwyn Hunt to be identified as the author of this work has been asserted by him in accordance with the Copyright, Designs and Patents Act 1988.

British Library Cataloguing in Publication Data
A catalogue record for this book is available from the British Library.

ISBN 1 84312 167 0

Typeset by Servis Filmsetting Ltd, Manchester
Printed and bound in Great Britain

Contents

Foreword

A child is impaired when a function of body or mind is not working properly, but a child is disabled when the physical or social environment prevents him or her from attaining his or her full potential as a person, as a pupil and as a young citizen.

While impairment is dealt with through rehabilitation and adaptive technology, disability is confronted through education, social awareness and political action. It is in the area of the educational environment, including the personal awareness of the teacher and the resources of the school, that Dilwyn Hunt's book makes an important contribution. This experienced expert shows how the social and educational impact of having special needs can be reduced and, sometimes, virtually eliminated.

Religious education in Europe today is at the centre of the search for human rights, especially in the area of full inclusion and the recognition and affirmation of difference. Hunt sets out in a clear and practical way the various kinds of disability the teacher is likely to encounter, and explains the most effective response to each special need.

I have known Dilwyn since the time when he was Head of the Religious Education Department in one of Birmingham's most progressive and innovative comprehensive schools, where he was a pioneer in approaches that included pupils from all faiths (and none) in the process of discovery. He brings to this book not only this experience but also his years of more recent work with schools and communities of many kinds in the West Midlands. His gifts of clarity, brevity and relevance make this book of great value to teachers and I am pleased to commend it.

John M. Hull
Emeritus Professor of Religious Education in the University of Birmingham
and Professor of Practical Theology in the Queen's Foundation for Ecumenical
Theological Education

April 2005

Acknowledgements

The author would like to thank:

Anthea Collinge, Dudley Wood School, Dudley

Christine Moorhouse, Castle High School, Dudley

Frank Bruce, Waverley School, Birmingham

Anne Mole, Kingswinford, Dudley

Heather Hughes, Cradley High School, Dudley

Carole Biggs, Educational Consultant

Lynn Openshaw, Behaviour and Attendance Consultant

Linda Raybould, Literacy Consultant

Permission to reproduce the following materials is gratefully acknowledged:

Daily Mail cover, p. 52, 'Playing God', courtesy of SOLO Syndication, London.

'Wall of Wisdom' (p. 53) and 'Mind Mapping' (p. 55) courtesy of *RE Today*.

Original line drawings by Iqbal Aslam and Jane Bottomley.

Contributors to the Series

The author

Dilwyn Hunt has been involved in teaching religious education for the last thirty years. He has written a variety of popular textbooks including the Leaders of Religion series published by Longmans and *Muslims 4,* which featured as part of the Westhill Project for RE 5-16. For the last ten years he has worked as a specialist RE adviser first in Birmingham and now in Dudley. He has a wide range of experience in the teaching of RE including mainstream and special RE.

Series editor

Alan Combes started teaching in South Yorkshire in 1967 and was Head of English at several secondary schools before taking on the role of Head of PSHE as part of being senior teacher at Pindar School, Scarborough. He took early retirement to focus on his writing career and has authored two citizenship textbooks as well as writing several features for the TES. He has been used as an adviser on citizenship by the DfES and has emphasised citizenship's importance for special needs pupils as a speaker for NASEN.

A dedicated team of SEN specialists and subject specialists have contributed to the *Meeting SEN in the Curriculum* series.

SEN specialists

Sue Briggs is a freelance education consultant based in Hereford. She writes and speaks on inclusion, special educational needs and disability, and Autistic Spectrum Disorders, and is a lay member of the SEN and Disability Tribunal. Until recently, she was SEN Inclusion Co-ordinator for Herefordshire Education Directorate. Originally trained as a secondary music teacher, Sue has extensive experience in mainstream and special schools. For six years she was teacher in charge of a language disorder unit.

Sue Cunningham is a learning support co-ordinator at a large mainstream secondary school in the West Midlands, where she manages a large team of learning support teachers and assistants. She has experience of working in both mainstream and special schools and has set up and managed a resource base for pupils with moderate learning difficulties in the mainstream as part of an initiative to promote a more inclusive education for pupils with SEN.

Sally McKeown has responsibility for language-based work in the Inclusion team at Becta. She has a particular interest in learning difficulties and dyslexia. She wrote the MFL Special Needs Materials for CILT's NOF training and is author of *Unlocking Potential* and co-author of *Supporting Children with Dyslexia* (Questions Publishing). She writes regularly for the TES, the *Guardian* and *Special Children* magazine.

Subject specialists

English

Tim Hurst has been a SEN co-ordinator in five schools and is particularly interested in the role and use of language in teaching.

Science

Carol Holden works as a science teacher and assistant SENCO in a mainstream secondary school. She has developed courses for pupils with SEN within science and has gained a graduate diploma and MA in Educational Studies, focusing on SEN.

History

Richard Harris has been teaching since 1989. He has taught in three comprehensive schools, as history teacher, head of department and head of faculty. He has also worked as teacher consultant for secondary history in West Berkshire.

Ian Luff is Assistant Headteacher of Kesgrave High School, Suffolk, and has been Head of History in three comprehensive schools.

Maths

Brian Sharp is a Key Stage 3 Mathematics consultant for Herefordshire. Brian has a long experience of working in both special and mainstream schools as a teacher of mathematics. He has a range of management experience, including SENCO, mathematics and ICT co-ordinator.

Music

Victoria Jaquiss is SEN specialist for music for children with emotional and behavioural difficulties in Leeds. She devised a system of musical notation primarily for use with steel pans, for which, in 2002, she was awarded the fellowship of the Royal Society of Arts.

Diane Paterson works as an inclusive music curriculum teacher in Leeds.

Geography

Diane Swift is a project leader for the Geographical Association. Her interest in special needs developed while she was a Staffordshire geography adviser and inspector.

PE and Sport

Crispin Andrews is an education/sports writer with nine years' experience of teaching and sports coaching.

Art

Kim Earle is Able Pupils Consultant for St Helens and has been a head of art and design. Kim is also a practising designer jeweller.

Gill Curry is Gifted and Talented Strand Co-ordinator for the Wirral. She has twenty years' experience as head of art and has also been an art advisory teacher. She is also a practising artist specialising in print.

ICT

Mike North works for ICTC, an independent consultancy specialising in the effective use of ICT in education. He develops educational materials and provides advice and support for the SEN sector.

Sally McKeown is an Education Officer with Becta, the government funded agency responsible for managing the National Grid for Learning and the FERL website. She is responsible for the use of IT for learners with disabilities, learning difficulties or additional needs.

Design and Technology

Louise T. Davies is Principal Officer for Design and Technology at Qualifications and Curriculum Authority, part-time, and also a freelance consultant. She is an experienced presenter and author of award-winning resources and books for schools. She chairs the Special Needs Advisory Group for the Design and Technology Association.

Citizenship

Alan Combes started teaching in South Yorkshire in 1967 and was Head of English at several secondary schools before taking on the role of Head of PSHE as part of being senior teacher at Pindar School, Scarborough. He took early retirement to focus on his writing career and has authored two citizenship text-books as well as writing several features for the *TES*. He has been used as an adviser on citizenship by the DfES and has emphasised citizenship's importance for special needs pupils as a speaker for NASEN.

Modern foreign languages

Sally McKeown is responsible for language-based work in the Inclusion team at Becta. She has a particular interest in learning difficulties and dyslexia. She writes regularly for the *TES, Guardian* and *Special Children* magazine.

Contents of the CD

The CD contains activities and record sheets which can be amended/individualised and printed out for use by the purchasing institution. Increasing the font size and spacing will improve accessibility for some students, as will changes in background colour. Alternatively, print out onto pastel-coloured paper for greater ease of reading.

Introduction

All children have the right to a good education and the opportunity to fulfil their potential. All teachers should expect to teach children with special educational needs (SEN) and all schools should play their part in educating children from the local community, whatever their background or ability. (*Removing Barriers to Achievement: The Government's Strategy for SEN*, February 2004)

A raft of legislation and statutory guidance over the past few years has sought to make our mainstream education system more inclusive and ensure that pupils with a diverse range of ability and need are well catered for. This means that all staff need to have an awareness of how children learn and develop in different ways and an understanding of how barriers to achievement can be removed – or at least minimised.

These barriers often result from inappropriate teaching styles, inaccessible teaching materials or ill-advised grouping of pupils, as much as from an individual child's physical, sensory or cognitive impairments: a fact which is becoming better understood. It is this developing understanding that is now shaping the legislative and advisory landscape of our education system, and exhorting all teachers to carefully consider their curriculum planning and classroom practice.

The major statutory requirements and non-statutory guidance are summarised in Chapter 1, setting the context for this resource and providing useful starting points for departmental INSET.

It is clear that provision for pupils with special educational needs is not the sole responsibility of the SENCO and his or her team of assistants. If, in the past, subject teachers have 'taken a back seat' in the planning and delivery of a suitable curriculum for these children and expected the Learning Support department to bridge the gap between what was on offer in the classroom, lab or studio and what they actually needed – they can no longer do so.

All teaching and non teaching staff should be involved in the development of the school's SEN policy and be fully aware of the school's procedure for identifying, assessing and making provision for pupils with SEN. (Table of Roles and Responsibilities, *Code of Practice*, DfES 2001)

Chapter 2 looks at departmental policy for SEN provision and provides useful audit material for reviewing and developing current practice.

The term 'special educational needs', or SEN, is now widely used and has become something of a catch-all descriptor – rendering it less than useful in many cases. Before the Warnock Report (1978) and subsequent introduction of the term 'special educational needs', any pupils who, for whatever reason (cognitive difficulties, emotional and behavioural difficulties, speech and language disorders), progressed more slowly than the 'norm' were designated 'remedials' and grouped together in the bottom sets, without the benefit, in many cases, of specialist subject teachers.

But the SEN tag was also applied to pupils in special schools who had more significant needs and had previously been identified as 'disabled' or even 'uneducable'. Add to these the deaf pupils, those with impaired vision, others with mobility problems, and even children from other countries, with a limited understanding of the English language – who may or may not have been highly intelligent – and you have a recipe for confusion to say the least.

The day-to-day descriptors used in the staffroom are gradually being moderated and refined as greater knowledge and awareness of special needs is built up. (We still hear staff describing pupils as 'totally thick', a 'nutcase' or 'complete moron' – but hopefully only as a means of letting off steam!) However, there are terms in common use which, though more measured and well-meaning, can still be unhelpful and misleading. Teachers will describe a child as being 'dyslexic' when they mean that he is poor at reading and writing; 'ADHD' has become a synonym for badly behaved; and a child who seems to be withdrawn or just eccentric is increasingly described as 'autistic'.

The whole process of applying labels is fraught with danger, but sharing a common vocabulary – and more importantly, a common understanding – can help colleagues to express their concerns about a pupil and address the issues as they appear in the classroom/lab/studio or on the sports field. Often, this is better achieved by identifying the particular areas of difficulty experienced by the pupil rather than puzzling over what syndrome he or she may have. The Code of Practice identifies four main areas of difficulty, and these are detailed in Chapter 3 – along with an 'at a glance' guide to a wide range of syndromes and conditions and guidance on how they might present barriers to learning.

There is no doubt that the number of children with special needs being educated in mainstream schools is growing:

> . . . because of the increased emphasis on the inclusion of children with SEN in mainstream schools the number of these children is increasing, as are the severity and variety of their SEN. Children with a far wider range of learning difficulties and variety of medical conditions, as well as sensory difficulties and physical disabilities, are now attending mainstream classes. The implication of this is that mainstream school teachers need to expand their knowledge and skills with regard to the needs of children with SEN. (Stakes and Hornby 2000: 3)

The continuing move to greater inclusion means that all teachers can now expect to teach pupils with varied, and quite significant, special educational needs at some time. Even five years ago, it was rare to come across children with Asperger's/Down's/Tourette's Syndrome, Autistic Spectrum Disorder or significant physical/sensory disabilities in community secondary schools. Now, they are entering mainstream education in growing numbers and there is a realisation that their 'inclusion' cannot be simply the responsibility of the SENCO and support staff. All staff have to be aware of particular learning needs and able to employ strategies in the classroom (and lab, studio, gym) that directly address those needs.

Chapter 4 considers the components of an inclusive classroom and how the physical environment and resources, structure of the lesson and teaching approaches can make a real difference to pupils with special needs. This theme is extended in Chapter 5 to look more closely at teaching and learning styles and consider ways in which to help all pupils maximise their potential.

The monitoring of pupils' achievements and progress is a key factor in identifying and meeting their learning needs. Those pupils who make slower progress than their peers are often working just as hard, or even harder, but their efforts can go unrewarded. Chapter 6 addresses the importance of target setting and subsequent assessment and review in acknowledging pupils' achievements and in showing the department's effectiveness in value-added terms.

Liaising with the SENCO and support staff is an important part of every teacher's role. The SENCO's status in a secondary school often means that this teacher is part of the leadership team and influential in shaping whole school policy and practice. Specific duties might include

- ensuring liaison with parents and other professionals;

- advising and supporting teaching and support staff;

- ensuring that appropriate Individual Education Plans are in place;

- ensuring that relevant background information about individual children with special educational needs is collected, recorded and updated;

- making plans for future support and setting targets for improvement;

- monitoring and reviewing action taken.

The SENCO has invariably undergone training in different aspects of special needs provision and has much to offer colleagues in terms of in-house training and advice about appropriate materials to use with pupils. The SENCO should be a frequent and valuable point of reference for all staff, but is often overlooked in this capacity. The presence of the SENCO at the occasional departmental meeting can be very effective in developing teachers' skills in relation to meeting SEN, making them aware of new initiatives and methodology and sharing information about individual children.

In most schools, however, the SENCO's skills and knowledge are channelled to the chalkface via a team of teaching or learning support assistants (TAs, LSAs). These assistants can be very able and well-qualified, but very underused in the classroom.

Chapter 7 looks at how teachers can manage in-class support in a way that makes the best use of a valuable resource.

Describing real-life situations with real pupils is a powerful way to demonstrate ideas and guidance. In Chapter 8, a number of case studies illustrate how different approaches can work.

The revised regulations for SEN provision make it clear that mainstream schools are expected to provide for pupils with a wide diversity of needs, and teaching is evaluated on the extent to which all pupils are engaged and enabled to achieve. This book has been produced in response to the implications of all of this for secondary subject teachers. It has been written by a religious education specialist with support from colleagues who have expertise within the SEN field so that the information and guidance given is both subject specific and pedagogically sound. The book and accompanying CD provide a resource that can be used with colleagues, to

- shape departmental policy and practice for special needs provision;

- enable staff to react with a measured response when inclusion issues arise;

- ensure that every pupil achieves appropriately in RE.

CHAPTER 1

Meeting Special Educational Needs – Your Responsibility

Inclusion in education involves the process of increasing the participation of students in, and reducing their exclusion from, the cultures, curricula and communities of local schools. (*Index for Inclusion*, 2000)

The *Index for Inclusion* was distributed to all maintained schools by the Department for Education and Skills and has been a valuable tool for many schools as they have worked to develop their inclusive practice. It supports schools in the review of their policies, practices and procedures, and the development of an inclusive approach, and where it has been used as part of the school improvement process – looking at inclusion in the widest sense – it has been a great success. For many people, however, the *Index* lacked any real teeth, and recent legislation and non-statutory guidance is more authoritative.

The SEN and Disability Act 2001

The Act amended the Disability Discrimination Act and created important new duties for schools:

- to take reasonable steps to ensure that disabled pupils are not placed at a substantial disadvantage in relation to the education and other services they provide. This means they must anticipate where barriers to learning lie and take action to remove them as far as they are able;

- to plan strategically to increase the extent to which disabled pupils can participate in the curriculum, make the physical environment more accessible and ensure that written material is provided in accessible formats.

The reasonable steps taken might include:

- changing policies and practices;

- changing course requirements;

- changing physical features of a building;

- providing interpreters or other support workers;

- delivering courses in alternative ways;

- providing materials in other formats.

A word needs to be said here about the special status of religious education within the curriculum. RE, like any other subject, has to meet the requirements of the SEN and Disability Act. So for example in order to ensure that 'written material is provided in accessible formats' an RE department might convert all their materials into an electronic form in order to ensure that they can easily be converted into large print or put into other alternative formats, such as Braille. In this way the department is anticipating 'reasonable adjustments' that might be needed.

Religious education, strictly speaking, is not part of the National Curriculum. However, it is a component of every maintained school's 'basic curriculum' and as such is bound by the requirements of the SEN and Disability legislation. All maintained schools, other than voluntary aided schools with a religious character, must teach RE according to a locally agreed syllabus. Some of agreed syllabuses contain information about the teaching of RE to young people with special education needs. However, many do not. Regardless of whether or not such information is in a local agreed syllabus, the principles of inclusion still apply to RE.

Voluntary aided schools of a religious character have to teach RE according to the school's trust deeds, or, as is more usually the case, according to the policy of the governors. An RE department in a voluntary aided school must also take reasonable steps to ensure that pupils with a special educational need are taught RE and must respond to the diverse learning needs of all pupils.

See Chapter 2 for further detail on SENDA and an INSET activity.

The Revised National Curriculum

The Revised National Curriculum (2002) emphasises the provision of effective learning opportunities for all learners and establishes three principles for promoting inclusion:

- the setting of suitable learning challenges;

- responding to pupils' diverse learning needs;

- overcoming potential barriers to learning and assessment.

The National Curriculum guidance suggests that staff may need to differentiate tasks and materials, and facilitate access to learning by:

- encouraging pupils to use all available senses and experiences;

- planning for participation in all activities;

- helping children to manage their behaviour, take part in learning and prepare for work;

- helping pupils to manage their emotions;

- giving teachers, where necessary, the discretion to teach pupils material from earlier key stages, providing consideration is given to age-appropriate learning contexts. This means that a fourteen-year-old with significant learning difficulties may be taught relevant aspects of the local agreed syllabuses programme of study for RE at KS3 , but at the same time working on suitable material founded in the PoS for Key Stage 1.

Most teachers of RE welcome and are very willing to respond to the principle of inclusion. However, there are some teachers of RE that have reservations about whether RE can effectively be taught to young people that have learning or physical difficulties. Such doubts give rise to a lack of will. The lack of will in the minds of some teachers forms probably the largest single obstacle to teaching RE to children with special educational needs.

The source of these reservations varies, but often they are linked to the belief that RE is a uniquely difficult subject. RE, it is sometimes thought, is particularly difficult because it requires young people to confront big questions about life. The *Non-Statutory National Framework for Religious Education* published by the DfES and QCA in 2004 (QCA/04/1336) refers to these big questions as 'ultimate questions' and, in a footnote, gives as examples, 'Is God real?', 'Why are we alive?', 'What is meant by good and evil?', 'Why do people suffer?' The suspicion in the minds of some teachers is that young people with learning difficulties have neither the interest nor the ability to consider such ultimate questions.

As a consequence of this, young people with learning difficulties may be given a highly diluted RE curriculum. The RE some young people with special educational needs receive avoids those aspects of religion which are seen as being deep and mysterious. Instead the RE curriculum is reduced to only the concrete and observable aspects of religious life like festivals, religious stories, pilgrimage, ceremonies and architecture. Under the mistaken belief that this is appropriate strategic planning enabling pupils to participate in the RE curriculum, young people with learning difficulties may hardly ever have opportunities to

- reflect on their own experience of life;

- interpret ideas or attempt to think about how they might have an application in their life;

- evaluate what they learn about religion;

- develop and communicate their own ideas.

In meeting the diverse learning needs of pupils, a balance has to be struck. The balance is between those concrete, factual aspects of an RE syllabus and those aspects of an RE syllabus which have to do with asking difficult questions. RE must help pupils not just to know facts about religion but to also have opportunities to learn from religion so that they can learn to understand, and gain the skills of interpretation, application and evaluation. But it is always a balance. It is never appropriate to abandon an essential part of RE for some children on the grounds that it is not appropriate for them. Achieving this balance means that we have to be inventive and find practical ways of supporting children with learning difficulties.

The Code of Practice for Special Educational Needs

The Revised Code of Practice (implemented in 2002) describes a cyclical process of planning, target setting and review for pupils with special educational needs. It also makes clear the expectation that the vast majority of pupils with special needs will be educated in mainstream settings. Those identified as needing over and above what the school can provide from its own resources, however, are nominated for 'School Action Plus', and outside agencies will be involved in planned intervention. This may involve professionals from the Learning Support Service, a specialist teacher or therapist, or an educational psychologist, working with the school's SENCO to put together an Individual Education Plan (IEP) for the pupil. In a minority of cases (the numbers vary widely between LEAs) pupils may be assessed by a multi-disciplinary team on behalf of the local education authority, whose representatives then decide whether or not to issue a Statement of SEN. This is a legally binding document detailing the child's needs and setting out the resources which should be provided. It is reviewed every year.

FUNDAMENTAL PRINCIPLES OF THE SPECIAL NEEDS CODE OF PRACTICE:

- A child with special educational needs should have their needs met.
- The special educational needs of children will normally be met in mainstream schools or settings.
- The views of the child should be sought and taken into account.
- Parents have a vital role to play in supporting their child's education.
- Children with special educational needs should be offered full access to a broad, balanced and relevant education, including an appropriate curriculum for the Foundation stage and the National Curriculum.

Ofsted

Ofsted inspectors are required to make judgements about a school's inclusion policy, and how this is translated into practice in individual classrooms. According to Ofsted (2003) the following key factors help schools to become more inclusive:

- a climate of acceptance of all pupils
- careful preparation of placements for SEN pupils

- availability of sufficient suitable teaching and personal support

- widespread awareness among staff of the particular needs of SEN pupils and an understanding of the practical ways of meeting these needs in the classroom

- sensitive allocation to teaching groups and careful curriculum modification, timetables and social arrangements

- availability of appropriate materials and teaching aids and adapted accommodation

- an active approach to personal and social development, as well as to learning

- well defined and consistently applied approaches to managing difficult behaviour

- assessment, recording and reporting procedures which can embrace and express adequately the progress of pupils with more complex SEN who make only small gains in learning and PSD

- involving parents/carers as fully as possible in decision-making, keeping them well informed about their child's progress and giving them as much practical support as possible

- developing and taking advantage of training opportunities, including links with special schools and other schools.

Policy into practice

Effective teaching for pupils with special educational needs is, by and large, effective for all pupils, but as schools become more inclusive, teachers need to be able to respond to a wider range of needs. The Government's strategy for SEN *Removing Barriers to Achievement* (DfES 2004) sets out ambitious proposals to 'help teachers expand their repertoire of inclusive skills and strategies and plan confidently to include children with increasingly complex needs'.

In many cases, pupils' individual needs will be met through greater differentiation of tasks and materials, i.e. school-based intervention as set out in the SEN Code of Practice. A smaller number of pupils may need access to specialist equipment and approaches or to alternative or adapted activities, as part of a 'School Action Plus' programme, augmented by advice and support from external specialists. The QCA website (2003) encourages teachers to take specific action to provide access to learning for pupils with special educational needs, by:

(a) providing for pupils who need help with communication, language and literacy, through

- using texts that pupils can read and understand

- using visual and written materials in different formats, including large print, symbol text and Braille

- using ICT, other technological aids and taped materials

- using alternative and augmentative communication, including signs and symbols

- using translators, communicators and amanuenses;

(b) planning, where necessary, to develop pupils' understanding through the use of all available senses and experiences, by

- using materials and resources that pupils can access through sight, touch, sound, taste or smell

- using word descriptions and other stimuli to make up for a lack of first-hand experiences

- using ICT, visual and other materials to increase pupils' knowledge of the wider world

- encouraging pupils to take part in everyday activities such as play, drama, class visits and exploring the environment;

(c) planning for pupils' full participation in learning and in physical and practical activities, by

- using specialist aids and equipment

- providing support from adults or peers when needed

- adapting tasks or environments

- providing alternative activities, where necessary;

(d) helping pupils to manage their behaviour, to take part in learning effectively and safely, and, at Key Stage 4, to prepare for work, by

- setting realistic demands and stating them explicitly

- using positive behaviour management, including a clear structure of rewards and sanctions

- giving pupils every chance and encouragement to develop the skills they need to work well with a partner or a group

- teaching pupils to value and respect the contribution of others

- encouraging and teaching independent working skills

- teaching essential safety rules;

(e) helping individuals to manage their emotions, particularly trauma or stress, and to take part in learning, by

- identifying aspects of learning in which the pupil will engage and planning short-term, easily achievable goals in selected activities

- providing positive feedback to reinforce and encourage learning and build self-esteem

- selecting tasks and materials sensitively to avoid unnecessary stress for the pupil

- creating a supportive learning environment in which the pupil feels safe and is able to engage with learning

- allowing time for the pupil to engage with learning and gradually increasing the range of activities and demands.

Pupils with disabilities

Not all pupils with disabilities will necessarily have special educational needs. Many learn alongside their peers with little need for additional resources beyond the aids which they use as part of their daily life, such as a wheelchair, a hearing aid or equipment to aid vision. Teachers' planning must ensure, however, that these pupils are enabled to participate as fully and effectively as possible in the curriculum by:

- planning appropriate amounts of time to allow for the satisfactory completion of tasks. This might involve:

- taking account of the very slow pace at which some pupils will be able to record work, either manually or with specialist equipment, and of the physical effort required

- being aware of the high levels of concentration necessary for some pupils when following or interpreting text or graphics, particularly when using vision aids or tactile methods, and of the tiredness which may result

- allocating sufficient time, opportunity and access to equipment for pupils to gain information through experimental work and detailed observation, including the use of microscopes

- being aware of the effort required by some pupils to follow oral work, whether through use of residual hearing, lip reading or a signer, and of the tiredness or loss of concentration which may occur;

- planning opportunities, where necessary, for the development of skills in practical aspects of the curriculum. This might involve:

- providing adapted, modified or alternative activities or approaches to learning in religious education and ensuring that these have integrity and equivalence to the local agreed syllabus and enable pupils to make appropriate progress

– providing alternative or adapted activities in science, art and design and design and technology for pupils who are unable to manipulate tools, equipment or materials or who may be allergic to certain types of materials

– ensuring that all pupils can be included and participate safely in geography field work, local studies and visits to museums, places of worship, historic buildings and sites;

● identifying aspects of programmes of study and attainment targets that may present specific difficulties for individuals. This might involve:

– using approaches to enable hearing impaired pupils to learn about sound in science and music

– helping visually impaired pupils to learn about light in science, to access maps and visual resources in geography and to evaluate different products in design and technology and images in art and design

– providing opportunities for pupils to develop strength in depth where they cannot meet the particular requirements of a subject, such as the visual requirements in art and design and the singing requirements in music

– discounting these aspects in appropriate individual cases when required to make a judgement against level descriptions.

Summary

Teachers are ultimately responsible for all the children they teach. In terms of participation, achievement, enjoyment – the buck stops here!

Pupils with a wide range of needs – physical/sensory, emotional, cognitive and social – are present in increasing numbers, in all mainstream settings.

Government policies point the way, with inclusion at the forefront of national policy – but it is up to teachers to make the rhetoric a reality.

Chapter 2 considers the departmental policy for special educational needs provision and inclusion, and how its development can shape classroom practice.

Departmental Policy

It is crucial that departmental policy describes a strategy for meeting pupils' special educational needs within the particular curricular area. The policy should set the scene for any visitor to the RE department – from supply staff to inspectors – and make a valuable contribution to the departmental handbook. The process of developing a department SEN policy offers the opportunity to clarify and evaluate current thinking and practice within the RE team and to establish a consistent approach.

The policy should:

- clarify the responsibilities of all staff and identify any with specialist training and/or knowledge;

- describe the curriculum on offer and how it can be differentiated;

- outline arrangements for assessment and reporting;

- guide staff on how to work effectively with support staff;

- identify staff training.

The starting point will be the school's SEN policy as required by the Education Act 1996, with each subject department 'fleshing out' the detail in a way which describes how things work in practice. The writing of a policy should be much more than a paper exercise completed to satisfy the senior management team and Ofsted inspectors. It is an opportunity for staff to come together as a team and create a framework for teaching RE in a way that makes it accessible to all pupils in the school.

Where to start when writing a policy?

An audit can act as a starting point for reviewing current policy on SEN or to inform the writing of a new policy. It will involve gathering information and reviewing current practice with regard to pupils with SEN and is best completed by the whole of the department, preferably with some additional advice from the SENCO or another member of staff with responsibility for SEN within the school. An audit carried out by the whole department can provide a valuable opportunity for professional development if it is seen as an exercise in sharing good practice and encouraging joint planning. But before embarking on an audit, it is worth investing some time in a department meeting or training day, to raise awareness of special educational needs legislation and establish a shared philosophy.

The following headings may be useful in establishing a working policy:

General statement

- What does legislation and DfES guidance say?

- What does the school policy state?

- What do members of the department have to do to comply with it?

Definition of SEN

- What does SEN mean?

- What are the areas of need and the categories used in the Code of Practice?

- Are there any special implications within the subject area?

Provision for staff within the department

- How is information shared?

- Who has responsibility for SEN within the department?

- How and when is information shared?

- Where and what information is stored?

Provision for pupils with SEN

- How are pupils with SEN assessed and monitored in the department?

- How are contributions to IEPs and reviews made?

- What criteria are used for organising teaching groups?

- What alternative courses are offered to pupils with SEN?

- What special internal and external examination arrangements are made?

- What guidance is available for working with support staff?

Resources and learning materials

- Is there any specialist equipment used in the department?

- How are resources developed?

- Where are resources stored?

Staff qualifications and Continuing Professional Development needs

- What qualifications do the members of the department have?

- What training has taken place?

- How is training planned?

- Is a record kept of training completed and training needs?

Monitoring and reviewing the policy

- How will the policy be monitored?

- When will the policy be reviewed?

The content of a SEN departmental policy

This section gives detailed information on what a SEN policy might include. Each heading is expanded with some detailed information and raises the main issues with regard to teaching pupils with SEN. At the end of each section there is an example statement. The example statements can be personalised and brought together to make a policy. All the examples in this chapter are gathered as an example policy in a 'Draft policy for SEN' on the CD.

General statement with reference to the school's SEN policy

All schools must have a SEN policy according to the Education Act 1996. This policy will set out basic information on the school's SEN provision, how the school identifies, assesses and provides for pupils with SEN, including information on staffing and working in partnership with other professionals and parents. Any department policy needs to have reference to the school SEN policy.

Example

> All members of the department will ensure that the needs of all pupils with SEN are met, according to the aims of the school and its SEN policy.

Definition of SEN

It is useful to insert at least the four areas of SEN in the department policy, as used in the Code of Practice for Special Educational Needs.

Example

Cognition and Learning Needs	Behaviour, Emotional and Social Development Needs	Communication and Interaction Needs	Sensory and/ or Physical Needs
Specific learning difficulties (SpLD)	Behaviour, emotional and social difficulties (BESD)	Speech, language and communication needs	Hearing impairment (HI)
Dyslexia	Attention Deficit Disorder (ADD)	Autistic Spectrum Disorder (ASD)	Visual impairment (VI)
Moderate learning difficulties (MLD)			
Severe learning difficulties (SLD)	Attention Deficit Hyperactivity Disorder (ADHD)	Asperger's Syndrome	Multi-sensory impairment (MSI)
Profound and multiple learning difficulties (PMLD)			Physical difficulties (PD)
			OTHER

Provision for staff within the department

In many schools, each department nominates a member of staff to have special responsibility for SEN provision (with or without remuneration). This can be very effective where there is a system of regular liaison between department SEN representatives and the SENCO in the form of meetings or paper communications or a mixture of both.

The responsibilities of this post may include liaison between the department and the SENCO, attending any liaison meetings and providing feedback via meetings and minutes, attending training, maintaining the departmental SEN information and records and representing the need of pupils with SEN at departmental level. This post can be seen as a valuable development opportunity for staff. The name of this person should be included in the policy.

Setting out how members of the department raise concerns about pupils with SEN can be included in this section. Concerns may be raised at specified departmental meetings before referral to the SENCO. An identified member of the department could make referrals to the SENCO and keep a record of this information.

Reference to working with support staff will include a commitment to planning and communication between staff. There may be information on inviting support staff to meetings, resources and lesson plans.

A reference to the centrally held lists of pupils with SEN and other relevant information will also be included in this section. A note about confidentiality of information should be included.

Example

> The member of staff with responsibility for overseeing the provision of SEN within the department will attend liaison meetings and feedback to other members of the department. He or she will maintain the department's SEN information file, attend appropriate training and disseminate this to all departmental staff. All information will be treated with confidentiality.

Provision for pupils with SEN

It is the responsibility of all staff to know which pupils have SEN and to identify any pupils having difficulties. Pupils with SEN may be identified by staff within the department in a variety of ways; these may be listed and could include:

- observation in lessons
- assessment of class work
- homework tasks
- end of module tests
- progress checks
- annual examinations
- reports.

Setting out how pupils with SEN are grouped within the RE department may include specifying the criteria used and/or the philosophy behind the method of grouping.

Example

> The pupils are grouped according to ability as informed by Key Stage 2 results, reading scores and any other relevant performance, social or medical information.

Monitoring arrangements and details of how pupils can move between groups should also be set out. Information collected may include:

- National Curriculum levels

- departmental assessments

- reading scores

- advice from pastoral staff

- discussion with staff in the SEN department

- information provided on IEPs.

Special Examination arrangements need to be considered not only at Key Stages 3 and 4 but also for internal examinations. How and when these will be discussed should be clarified. Reference to SENCO and examination arrangements from the examination board should be taken into account. Recognition that staff in the department understand the current legislation and guidance from central government is important, so a reference to the SEN Code of Practice and the levels of SEN intervention is helpful within the policy. Here is a good place also to put a statement about the school behaviour policy and rewards and sanctions and how the department will make any necessary adjustments to meet the needs of pupils with SEN.

Example

It is understood that pupils with SEN may receive additional support if they have a Statement of SEN, or are at School Action Plus or School Action. The staff in the RE department will aim to support the pupils to achieve their targets as specified on their IEPs and will provide feedback for IEP or Statement reviews. Pupils with SEN will be included in the departmental monitoring system used for all pupils. Additional support will be requested as appropriate.

Resources and learning materials

The department policy needs to specify what differentiated materials are available, where they are kept and how to find new resources. This section could include a statement about working with support staff to develop resources or access specialist resources as needed and the use of ICT. Teaching strategies may also be identified if appropriate. Advice on more specialist equipment can be sought as necessary, possibly through LEA support services: contact details may be available from the SENCO, or the department may have direct links. Any specially bought subject text or alternative/appropriate courses can be specified as well as any external assessment and examination courses.

Example

> The department will provide suitably differentiated materials and, where appropriate, specialist resources for pupils with SEN. Additional texts are available for those pupils working below National Curriculum level 3. At Key Stage 4 an alternative course to GCSE is offered at Entry level, but where possible pupils with SEN will be encouraged to reach their full potential and follow a GCSE course. Support staff will be provided with curriculum information in advance of lessons and will also be involved in lesson planning. A list of resources is available in the department handbook and on the noticeboard.

Staff qualifications and Continuing Professional Development needs

It is important to recognise and record the qualifications and special skills gained by staff within the department. Training can include not only external courses but also in-house INSET and opportunities such as observing other staff, working to produce materials with other staff, and visiting other establishments. Staff may have hidden skills that might enhance the work of the department and the school; for example, some staff might be proficient in the use of sign language.

Example

> A record of training undertaken, specialist skills, and training required, will be kept in the department handbook. Requests for training will be considered in line with the department and school improvement plan.

Monitoring and reviewing the policy

Any policy to be effective needs regular monitoring and review. These can be planned as part of the yearly cycle. The responsibility for the monitoring can rest with the Head of Department but will have more effect if supported by someone from outside acting as a critical friend, this could be the SENCO or a member of the senior management team in school.

Example

> The department SEN policy will be monitored by the Head of Department on a planned annual basis, with advice being sought from the SENCO as part of a three-yearly review process.

Summary

Creating a departmental SEN policy should be a developmental activity to improve the teaching and learning for all pupils but especially those with special or additional needs. The policy should be a working document that will evolve and change; it is there to challenge current practice and to encourage improvement for both pupils and staff. If departmental staff work together to create the policy, they will have ownership of it; it will have true meaning and be effective in clarifying practice.

Activity 1

WHAT DO WE REALLY THINK?

Each member of the department should choose two of these statements and pin them on to the noticeboard for an overview of staff opinion. The person leading the session (Head of Department, SENCO, senior manager) should be ready to address any negative feedback and take forward the department in a positive approach.

If my own child had special needs, I would want her/him to be in a mainstream school mixing with all sorts of kids.

I want to be able to cater for pupils with SEN but feel that I don't have the expertise required.

Special needs kids in mainstream schools are all right up to a point, but I didn't sign up for dealing with the more severe problems – they should be in special schools.

It is the SENCO's responsibility to look out for these pupils with SEN – with help from support teachers.

Pupils with special needs should be catered for the same as any others. Teachers can't pick and choose the pupils they want to teach.

I need much more time to plan if pupils with SEN are going to be coming to my lessons.

Big schools are just not the right places for blind or deaf kids, or those in wheelchairs.

I would welcome more training on how to provide for pupils with SEN in RE.
I have enough to do without worrying about kids who can't read or write.

If their behaviour distracts other pupils in any way, youngsters with SEN should be withdrawn from the class.

N.B. A sheet listing the main points from SENDA is included as Appendix 1.

CHAPTER 3

Different Types of SEN

This chapter is a starting point for information on the special educational needs most frequently occurring in the mainstream secondary school. It describes the main characteristics of each learning difficulty with practical ideas for use in subject areas, and contacts for further information. Some of the tips are based on good secondary practice while others encourage teachers to try new or less familiar approaches.

The special educational needs in this chapter are grouped under the headings used in the SEN *Code of Practice* (DfES 2001):

- cognition and learning

- behaviour, emotional and social development

- communication and interaction

- sensory and/or physical needs.
  (see p. 16)

The labels used in this chapter are useful when describing pupils' difficulties, but it is important to remember not to use the label in order to define the pupil. Put the pupil before the difficulty, saying 'the pupil with special educational needs' rather than 'the SEN pupil'; 'pupils with MLD' rather than 'MLDs'.

Remember to take care in using labels when talking with parents, pupils or other professionals. Unless a pupil has a firm diagnosis, and parents and pupil understand the implications of that diagnosis, it is more appropriate to describe the features of the special educational need rather than use the label. For example a teacher might describe a pupil's spelling difficulties but not use the term 'dyslexic'.

The number and profile of pupils with special educational needs will vary from school to school, so it is important to consider the pupil with SEN as an individual within your school and subject environment. The strategies contained in this chapter will help teachers adapt that environment to meet the needs of individual pupils within the subject context. For example, rather than saying, 'He can't read the worksheet', recognise that the worksheet is too difficult for the pupil, and adapt the work accordingly.

There is a continuum of need within each of the special educational needs listed here. Some pupils will be affected more than others, and show fewer or more of the characteristics described.

The availability and levels of support from professionals within a school (e.g. SENCOs, support teachers, teaching assistants) and external professionals (e.g. educational psychologists, Learning Support Service staff, medical staff) will depend on the severity of pupils' SEN. This continuum of need will also impact on the subject teacher's planning and allocation of support staff.

Pupils with other less common special educational needs may be included in some secondary schools, and additional information on these conditions may be found in a variety of sources. These include the school SENCO, LEA support services, educational psychologists and the internet.

Asperger's Syndrome

Asperger's Syndrome is a disorder at the able end of the autistic spectrum. People with Asperger's Syndrome have average to high intelligence but share the same Triad of Impairments. They often want to make friends but do not understand the complex rules of social interaction. They have impaired fine and gross motor skills, with writing being a particular problem. Boys are more likely to be affected – with the ratio being 10:1 boys to girls. Because they appear 'odd' and naive, these pupils are particularly vulnerable to bullying.

Main characteristics

- **Social interaction**
  Pupils with Asperger's Syndrome want friends but have not developed the strategies necessary for making and sustaining friendships. They find it very difficult to learn social norms and to pick up on social cues. Highly social situations, such as lessons, can cause great anxiety.
- **Social communication**
  Pupils have appropriate spoken language but tend to sound formal and pedantic, using little expression and with an unusual tone of voice. They have difficulty using and understanding non-verbal language such as facial expression, gesture, body language and eye-contact. They have a literal understanding of language and do not grasp implied meanings.
- **Social imagination**
  Pupils with Asperger's Syndrome need structured environments, and to have routines they understand and can anticipate. They excel at learning facts and figures, but have difficulty understanding abstract concepts and in generalising information and skills. They often have all-consuming special interests.

How can the RE teacher help?

- Liaise closely with parents, especially over homework.
- Create as calm a classroom environment as possible.
- Allow to sit in the same place for each lesson.
- Set up a 'work buddy' system for your lessons.
- Provide additional visual cues in class.
- Give time to process questions and respond.
- Make sure pupils understand what to do.
- Allow alternatives to writing for recording.
- Use visual timetables and task activity lists.
- Prepare for changes to routines well in advance.
- Give written homework instructions and stick into an exercise book.
- Have your own class rules and apply them consistently.

The National Autistic Society, 393 City Road, London ECIV 1NG
Tel: 0870 600 8585 Helpline (10am–4pm, Mon–Fri) Tel: 020 7833 2299
Fax: 020 7833 9666 Email: nas@nas.org.uk Website: www.nas.org.uk

Attention Deficit Disorder (with or without Hyperactivity) – ADD/ADHD

Attention Deficit Hyperactivity Disorder is a term used to describe children who exhibit over-active behaviour and impulsivity and who have difficulty in paying attention. This is caused by a form of brain dysfunction of a genetic nature. ADHD can sometimes be controlled effectively by medication. Children of all levels of ability can have ADHD.

Main characteristics

- difficulty in following instructions and completing tasks
- easily distracted by noise, movement of others, objects attracting attention
- often doesn't listen when spoken to
- fidgets and becomes restless, can't sit still
- interferes with other pupils' work
- can't stop talking, interrupts others, calls out
- runs about when inappropriate
- has difficulty in waiting or taking turns
- acts impulsively without thinking about the consequences.

How can the RE teacher help?

- Make eye contact and use the pupil's name when speaking to him.
- Keep instructions simple – the one-sentence rule.
- Provide clear routines and rules, rehearse them regularly.
- Sit the pupil away from obvious distractions, e.g. windows, the computer.
- In busy situations direct the pupil by name to visual or practical objects.
- Encourage the pupil to repeat back instructions before starting work.
- Tell the pupil when to begin a task.
- Give two choices, avoid the option of the pupil saying 'no': 'Do you want to write in blue or black pen?'
- Give advance warning when something is about to happen, change or finish with a time, e.g. 'In two minutes I need you (pupil name) to . . .'
- Give specific praise – catch him being good, give attention for positive behaviour.
- Give the pupil responsibilities so that others can see him in a positive light and he develops a positive self-image.

ADD Information Services, PO Box 340, Edgware, Middlesex, HA8 9HL
Tel: 020 8906 9068
ADDNET UK www.btinternet.com/~black.ice/addnet/

Autistic Spectrum Disorders (ASD)

The term 'Autistic Spectrum Disorders' (ASD) is used for a range of disorders affecting the development of social interaction, social communication and social imagination and flexibility of thought. This is known as the 'Triad of Impairments'. Pupils with ASD cover the full range of ability, and the severity of the impairment varies widely. Some pupils also have learning disabilities or other difficulties. Four times as many boys as girls are diagnosed with an ASD.

Main characteristics

- **Social interaction**
  Pupils with an ASD find it difficult to understand social behaviour, and this affects their ability to interact with children and adults. They do not always understand social contexts. They may experience high levels of stress and anxiety in settings that do not meet their needs or when routines are changed. This can lead to inappropriate behaviour.

- **Social communication**
  Understanding and use of non-verbal and verbal communication is impaired. Pupils with an ASD have difficulty understanding the communication of others and in developing effective communication themselves. They have a literal understanding of language. Many are delayed in learning to speak, and some never develop speech at all.

- **Social imagination and flexibility of thought**
  Pupils with an ASD have difficulty in thinking and behaving flexibly, which may result in restricted, obsessional or repetitive activities. They are often more interested in objects than people, and have intense interests in such things as trains and vacuum cleaners. Pupils work best when they have a routine. Unexpected changes in those routines will cause distress. Some pupils with Autistic Spectrum Disorders have a different perception of sounds, sights, smell, touch and taste, and this can affect their response to these sensations.

How can the RE teacher help?

- Liaise with parents as they will have many useful strategies.

- Provide visual supports in class: objects, pictures, etc.

- Give a symbolic or written timetable for each day.

- Give advance warning of any changes to usual routines.

- Provide either an individual desk or a work buddy.

- Avoid using too much eye contact as it can cause distress.

- Give individual instructions using the pupil's name, e.g. 'Paul, bring me your book.'

- Allow access to computers.

- Develop social interactions using a buddy system or Circle of Friends.

- Avoid using metaphor, idiom or sarcasm – say what you mean in simple language.

- Use special interests to motivate.

- Allow difficult situations to be rehearsed by means of Social Stories.

BEHAVIOURAL, EMOTIONAL AND SOCIAL DEVELOPMENT NEEDS

This term includes behavioural, emotional, social difficulties and Attention Deficit Disorder with or without Hyperactivity. These difficulties can be seen across the whole ability range and have a continuum of severity. Pupils with special educational needs in this category are those that have persistent difficulties despite an effective school behaviour policy and a personal and social curriculum.

Behavioural, emotional and social difficulties (BESD)

Main characteristics

- inattentive, poor concentration and lacks interest in school/school work
- easily frustrated, anxious about changes
- unable to work in groups
- unable to work independently, constantly seeking help
- confrontational – verbally aggressive towards pupils and/or adults
- physically aggressive towards pupils and/or adults
- destroys property – their own/others
- appears withdrawn, distressed, unhappy, sulky, may self-harm
- lacks confidence, acts extremely frightened, lacks self-esteem
- finds it difficult to communicate
- finds it difficult to accept praise.

How can the RE teacher help?

- Check the ability level of the pupil and adapt the level of work to this.
- Consider the pupil's strengths and use them.
- Tell the pupil what you expect in advance, for work and behaviour.
- Talk to the pupil to find out a bit about them.
- Set a subject target with a reward system.
- Focus your comments on the behaviour not on the pupil, and offer an alternative way of behaving when correcting the pupil.
- Use positive language and verbal praise whenever possible.
- Tell the pupil what you want them to do 'I need you to . . .' 'I want you to . . .' rather than ask. This avoids confrontation and the possibility that there is room for negotiation.
- Give the pupil a choice between two options.
- Stick to what you say.
- Involve the pupil in responsibilities to increase self-esteem and confidence.
- Plan a 'time out' system; ask a colleague for help with this.

Cerebral palsy (CP)

Cerebral palsy is a persistent disorder of movement and posture. It is caused by damage or lack of development to part of the brain before or during birth or in early childhood. Problems vary from slight clumsiness to more severe lack of control of movements. Pupils with CP may also have learning difficulties. They may use a wheelchair or other mobility aid.

Main characteristics

There are three main forms of cerebral palsy:

- *spasticity* – disordered control of movement associated with stiffened muscles

- *athetosis* – frequent involuntary movements

- *ataxia* – an unsteady gait with balance difficulties and poor spatial awareness.

  Pupils may also have communication difficulties.

How can the RE teacher help?

- Talk to parents, the physiotherapist – and the pupil.

- Consider the classroom layout.

- Have high academic expectations.

- Use visual supports: objects, pictures, symbols.

- Arrange a work/subject buddy.

- Speak directly to the pupil rather than through a teaching assistant.

- Ensure access to appropriate IT equipment for the subject – and that it is used.

Scope, PO BOX 833, Milton Keynes MK12 5NY
Tel: 0808 800 3333 (Freephone helpline) Fax: 01908 321051
Email: cphelpline@scope.org.uk Website: www.scope.org.uk

Down's Syndrome (DS)

Down's Syndrome (DS) is the most common identifiable cause of learning disability. This is a genetic condition caused by the presence of an extra chromosome 21. People with DS have varying degrees of learning difficulties ranging from mild to severe. They have a specific learning profile with characteristic strengths and weaknesses. All share certain physical characteristics but will also inherit family traits, in physical features and personality. They may have additional sight, hearing, respiratory and heart problems.

Main characteristics

- delayed motor skills

- taking longer to learn and consolidate new skills

- limited concentration

- difficulties with generalisation, thinking and reasoning

- sequencing difficulties

- stronger visual than aural skills

- better social than academic skills.

How can the RE teacher help?

- Sit where best able to see and hear.

- Speak directly to pupil and reinforce with facial expression, pictures and objects.

- Use simple, familiar language in short sentences.

- Check instructions have been understood.

- Give time to process information and formulate a response.

- Break lessons up into a series of shorter, varied and achievable tasks.

- Accept other ways of recording: drawings, tape/video recordings, symbols, etc.

- Set differentiated tasks linked to the work of the rest of the class.

- Provide age-appropriate resources and activities.

- Allow working in top sets to give good behaviour models.

- Provide a 'work buddy'.

- Expect unsupported work for part of each lesson.

The Down's Association, 155 Mitcham Road, London SW17 9PG
Tel: 020 8682 4001
Email: info@downs-syndrome.org.uk
Website: www.downs-syndrome.org.uk

Fragile X Syndrome

Fragile X Syndrome is caused by a malformation of the X chromosome and is the most common form of inherited learning disability. This intellectual disability varies widely with up to a third having learning problems ranging from moderate to severe. More boys than girls are affected, but both may be carriers.

Main characteristics

- delayed and disordered speech and language development
- difficulties with the social use of language
- articulation and/or fluency difficulties
- verbal skills better developed than reasoning skills
- repetitive or obsessive behaviour such as hand-flapping, chewing, etc.
- clumsiness and fine motor co-ordination problems
- attention deficit and hyperactivity
- easily anxious or overwhelmed in busy environments.

How can the RE teacher help?

- Liaise with parents.
- Make sure the pupil knows what is to happen in each lesson – provide visual timetables, work schedules or written lists.
- Ensure the pupil sits at the front of class, in the same seat for all lessons.
- Arrange a work/subject buddy.
- Where possible, keep to routines and give prior warning of all changes.
- Make instructions clear and simple.
- Use visual supports: objects, pictures, symbols.
- Allow the pupil to use a computer to record and access information.
- Give lots of praise and positive feedback.

Fragile X Society, Rood End House, 6 Stortford Road, Dunmow, Essex CM6 1DA
Tel: 01434 813147 (Helpline) Tel: 01371 875100 (Office)
Email: info@fragilex.org.uk Website: www.fragilex.org.uk

Moderate learning difficulties (MLD)

The term 'moderate learning difficulties' is used to describe pupils who find it extremely difficult to achieve expected levels of attainment across the curriculum even with a differentiated and flexible approach. These pupils do not find learning easy and can suffer from low self-esteem, and sometime exhibit unacceptable behaviour as a way of avoiding failure.

Main characteristics

- difficulties with reading, writing and comprehension
- unable to understand and retain basic mathematical skills and concepts
- immature social and emotional skills
- limited vocabulary and communication skills
- short attention span
- underdeveloped co-ordination skills
- lack of logical reasoning
- inability to transfer and apply skills to different situations
- difficulty remembering what has been taught
- difficulty with organising themselves, following a timetable, remembering books and equipment.

How can the RE teacher help?

- Check the pupil's strengths, weaknesses and attainment levels.
- Establish a routine within the lesson.
- Keep tasks short and varied.
- Keep listening tasks short or broken up with activities.
- Provide word lists, writing frames, shorten text.
- Try alternative methods of recording information, e.g. drawings, charts, labelling, diagrams, use of ICT.
- Check previously gained knowledge and build on this.
- Repeat information in different ways.
- Show the child what to do or what the expected outcome is; demonstrate or show examples of completed work.
- Use practical, concrete, visual examples to illustrate explanations.

- Question the pupil to check they have grasped a concept or can follow instructions.

- Make sure the pupil always has something to do.

- Use lots of praise, instant rewards, catch them trying hard.

The MLD Alliance, c/o The Elfrida Society, 34 Islington Park Street, London N1 1PX
www.mldalliance.com/executive.htm

Physical disability (PD)

There is a wide range of physical disabilities (PD), and pupils with PD cover all academic abilities. Some pupils are able to access the curriculum and learn effectively without additional educational provision. They have a disability but do not have a special educational need. For other pupils the impact on their education may be severe, and the school will need to make adjustments to enable them to access the curriculum.

Some pupils with a physical disability have associated medical conditions which may impact on their mobility. These include cerebral palsy, heart disease, spina bifida and hydrocephalus, and muscular dystrophy. Pupils with physical disabilities may also have sensory impairments, neurological problems or learning difficulties. They may use a wheelchair and/or additional mobility aids. Some pupils will be mobile but may have significant fine motor difficulties which require support. Others may need augmentative or alternative communication aids.

Pupils with a physical disability may need to miss lessons to attend physiotherapy or medical appointments. They are also likely to become very tired as they expend greater effort to complete everyday tasks. Schools will need to be flexible and sensitive to individual pupil needs.

How can the RE teacher help?

- Get to know pupils and parents and they will help you make the right adjustments.

- Maintain high expectations.

- Consider the classroom layout.

- Allow the pupil to leave lessons a few minutes early to avoid busy corridors and give time to get to next lesson.

- Set homework earlier in the lesson so instructions are not missed.

- Speak directly to the pupil rather than through a teaching assistant.

- Let pupils make their own decisions.

- Ensure access to appropriate IT equipment for the lesson – and that it is used!

- Give alternative ways of recording work.

- Plan to cover work missed through medical or physiotherapy appointments.

- Be sensitive to fatigue, especially at the end of the school day.

Semantic Pragmatic Disorder (SPD)

Semantic Pragmatic Disorder is a communication disorder which falls within the autistic spectrum. Semantic refers to the meanings of words and phrases and pragmatic refers to the use of language in a social context. Pupils with this disorder have difficulties understanding the meaning of what people say and using language to communicate effectively. Pupils with SPD find it difficult to extract the central meaning – saliency – of situations.

Main characteristics

- delayed language development
- fluent speech but may sound stilted or over-formal
- may repeat phrases out of context from videos or adult conversations
- difficulty understanding abstract concepts
- limited or inappropriate use of eye contact, facial expression or gesture
- motor skills problems.

How can the subject teacher help?

- Sit the pupil at the front of the room to avoid distractions.
- Use visual supports: objects, pictures, symbols.
- Pair with a work/subject buddy.
- Create a calm working environment with clear classroom rules.
- Be specific and unambiguous when giving instructions.
- Make sure instructions are understood, especially when using subject-specific vocabulary that can have another meaning in a different context.

AFASIC, 2nd Floor, 50–52 Great Sutton Street, London EC1V 0DJ
Tel: 0845 355 5577 (Helpline) (11 a.m. to 2 p.m.) Tel: 020 7490 9410
Fax: 020 7251 2834
Email: info@afasic.org.uk
Website: www.afasic.org.uk

Sensory impairments

Hearing impairment (HI)

The term 'hearing impairment' is a generic term used to describe all hearing loss. The main types of loss are monaural, conductive, sensory and mixed loss. The degree of hearing loss is described as mild, moderate, severe or profound. Some children rely on lip reading, others will use hearing aids and a small proportion will have British Sign Language (BSL) as their primary means of communication.

How can the RE teacher help?

- Check the degree of loss the pupil has.

- Check the best seating position (e.g. away from the hum of OHP and computers, with good ear to speaker).

- Check that the pupil can see your face for facial expressions and lip reading.

- Provide a list of vocabulary, context and visual clues, especially for new subjects.

- During class discussion allow one pupil to speak at a time and indicate where the speaker is.

- check that any aids are working, and if there is any other specialist equipment available.

Royal National Institute for the Deaf (RNID), 19–23 Featherstone St, London EC1Y 8SL Tel: 0808 808 0123
British Deaf Association (BDA) 1–3 Worship St, London EC2A 2AB
British Association of Teachers of the Deaf (BATOD), The Orchard, Leven,
North Humberside, HU17 5QA
www.batod.org.uk

Visual impairment (VI)

Visual impairment refers to a range of difficulties including those pupils with monocular vision (vision in one eye), those who are partially sighted and those who are blind. Pupils with visual impairment cover the whole ability range and some pupils may have other SEN.

How can the RE teacher help?

- Check the optimum position for the pupil, e.g. for a monocular pupil their good eye should be towards the action.
- Always provide the pupil with their own copy of the text.
- Provide enlarged-print copies of written text.
- Check use of ICT (enlarged icons, talking text, teach keyboard skills).
- Do not stand with your back to the window as this creates a silhouette and makes it harder for the pupil to see you.
- Draw the pupil's attention to displays – which they may not notice.
- Make sure the floor is kept free of clutter.
- Tell the pupil if there is a change to the layout of a space.
- Ask if there is any specialist equipment available (enlarged print dictionaries, lights).

Royal National Institute of the Blind, 105 Judd Street, London WC1H 9NE
Tel: 020 7388 1266 Fax: 020 7388 2034
Website: www.rnib.org.uk

Multi-sensory impairment

Pupils with multi-sensory impairment have a combination of visual and hearing difficulties. They may also have other additional disabilities that make their situation complex. A pupil with these difficulties is likely have a high level of individual support.

How can the RE teacher help?

- The subject teacher will need to liaise with support staff to ascertain the appropriate provision within each subject.

- Consideration will need to be given to alternative means of communication.

- Be prepared to be flexible and to adapt tasks, targets and assessment procedures.

Severe learning difficulties (SLD)

This term covers a wide and varied group of pupils who have significant intellectual or cognitive impairments. Many have communication difficulties and/or sensory impairments in addition to more general cognitive impairments. They may also have difficulties in mobility, co-ordination and perception. Some pupils may use signs and symbols to support their communication and understanding. Their attainments may be within or below level 1 of the National Curriculum, or in the upper P scale range (P4–P8), for much of their school careers.

How can the RE teacher help?

- Liaise with parents.

- Arrange a work/subject buddy.

- Use visual supports: objects, pictures, symbols.

- Learn some signs relevant to the subject.

- Allow time to process information and formulate responses.

- Set differentiated tasks linked to the work of the rest of the class.

- Set achievable targets for each lesson or module of work.

- Accept different recording methods: drawings, audio or video recordings, photographs, etc.

- Give access to computers where appropriate.

- Give a series of short, varied activities within each lesson.

Profound and multiple learning difficulties (PMLD)

Pupils with profound and multiple learning difficulties (PMLD) have complex learning needs. In addition to very severe learning difficulties, pupils have other significant difficulties, such as physical disabilities, sensory impairments or severe medical conditions. Pupils with PMLD require a high level of adult support, both for their learning needs and for their personal care.

They are able to access the curriculum through sensory experiences and stimulation. Some pupils communicate by gesture, eye pointing or symbols, others by very simple language. Their attainments are likely to remain in the early P scale range (P1–P4) throughout their school careers (that is below level 1 of the National Curriculum). The P scales provide small, achievable steps to monitor progress. Some pupils will make no progress or may even regress because of associated medical conditions. For this group experiences are as important as attainment.

How can the RE teacher help?

- Liaise with parents and teaching assistants.

- Consider the classroom layout.

- Identify possible sensory experiences in your lessons.

- Use additional sensory supports: objects, pictures, fragrances, music, movements, food, etc.

- Take photographs to record experiences and responses.

- Set up a work/subject buddy rota for the class.

- Identify times when the pupil can work with groups.

MENCAP, 117–123 Golden Lane, London EC1Y 0RT
Tel: 020 7454 0454 Website: www.mencap.org.uk

SPECIFIC LEARNING DIFFICULTIES (SpLD)

The term 'specific learning difficulties' covers dyslexia, dyscalculia and dyspraxia.

Dyslexia

The term 'dyslexia' is used to describe a learning difficulty associated with words, and it can affect a pupil's ability to read, write and/or spell. Research has shown that there is no one definitive definition of dyslexia or one identified cause, and it has a wide range of symptoms. Although found across a whole range of ability levels the idea that dyslexia presents as a difficulty between expected outcomes and performance is widely held.

Main characteristics

- In reading, the pupil may frequently lose their place, make frequent errors with the high-frequency words, have difficulty reading names, have difficult blending sounds and segmenting words. Reading requires a great deal of effort and concentration.

- In writing, the pupil's work may seem messy with crossing-outs; similarly shaped letters may be confused such as b/d, p/q, m/w, n/u, and letters in words may be jumbled – tired/tried. Spelling difficulties often persist into adult life, and these pupils become reluctant writers.

How can the RE teacher help?

- Be aware of the type of difficulty and the pupil's strengths.

- Teach and allow the use of word processing, spellcheckers and computer-aided learning packages.

- Provide word lists and photocopies of copying from the board.

- Consider alternative recording methods, e.g. pictures, plans, flow charts, mind maps.

- Allow extra time for tasks, including assessments and examinations.

The British Dyslexia Association
Tel: 0118 966 8271 www.bda-dyslexia.org.uk
Dyslexia Institute
Tel: 07184 463851 www.dyslexia-inst.org.uk

Dyscalculia

The term 'dyscalculia' is used to describe a difficulty in mathematics. This might be either a marked discrepancy between the pupil's developmental level and general ability on measures of specific maths ability or a total inability to abstract or consider concepts and numbers.

Main characteristics

- *In number*, the pupil may have difficulty counting by rote, writing or reading numbers, may miss out or reverse numbers, and have difficulty with mental maths, and be unable to remember concepts, rules and formulae.

- *In maths based concepts*, the pupil may have difficulty with money, telling the time, with directions, right and left, with sequencing events or losing track of turns, e.g. in team games, or dance.

How can the RE teacher help?

- Provide number/word/rule/formulae lists and photocopies of copying from the board.

- Make use of ICT and teach the use of calculators.

- Encourage the use of rough paper for working out.

- Plan the setting out of work, with it well spaced on the page.

- Provide practical objects that are age appropriate to aid learning.

- Allow extra time for tasks, including assessments and examinations.

Website: www.dyscalculia.co.uk.

Dyspraxia

The term 'dyspraxia' is used to describe an immaturity with the way in which the brain processes information, resulting in messages not being properly transmitted.

Main characteristics

- difficulty in co-ordinating movements, may appear awkward and clumsy
- difficulty with handwriting and drawing, throwing and catching
- difficulty following sequential events, e.g. multiple instructions
- tendency to misinterpret situations, take things literally
- limited social skills, leading to frustration and irritability
- some articulation difficulties (see verbal dyspraxia).

How can the RE teacher help?

- Be sensitive to the pupil's limitations in games and outdoor activities and plan tasks to enable success.
- Ask the pupil questions to check his understanding of instructions/tasks.
- Check seating position to encourage good presentation (both feet resting on the floor, desk at elbow height and with ideally a sloping surface to work on).

Dyspraxic Foundation, 8 West Alley, Hitchin, Herts SG5 1EG
Tel: 01462 454986 www.dyspraxiafoundation.org.uk

Speech, language and communication difficulties (SLCD)

Pupils with speech, language and communication difficulties (SLCD) have problems understanding what others say and/or making others understand what they say. Their development of speech and language skills may be significantly delayed. Speech and language difficulties are very common in young children, but most problems are resolved during the primary years. Problems that persist beyond the transfer to secondary school will be more severe. Any problem affecting speech, language and communication will have a significant effect on a pupil's self-esteem and personal and social relationships. The development of literacy skills is also likely to be affected. Even where pupils learn to decode, they may not understand what they have read. Sign language gives pupils an additional method of communication. Pupils with speech, language and communication difficulties cover the whole range of academic abilities.

Main characteristics

- **Speech difficulties**
  Pupils who have difficulties with expressive language may experience problems in articulation and the production of speech sounds, or in co-ordinating the muscles that control speech. They may have a stammer or some other form of dysfluency.
- **Language/communication difficulties**
  Pupils with receptive language impairments have difficulty understanding the meaning of what others say. They may use words incorrectly with inappropriate grammatical patterns, have a reduced vocabulary, or find it hard to recall words and express ideas. Some pupils will also have difficulty using and understanding eye-contact, facial expression, gesture and body language.

How can the RE teacher help?

- Talk to parents, speech therapist – and the pupil.
- Learn the most common signs for your subject.
- Use visual supports: objects, pictures, symbols.
- Use the pupil's name when addressing them.
- Give one instruction at a time, using short, simple sentences.
- Give time to respond before repeating a question.
- Make sure pupils understand what they have to do before starting a task.
- Pair the pupil with a work/subject buddy.
- Give access to a computer or other IT equipment appropriate to the subject.
- Give written homework instructions.

ICAN, 4 Dyer's Buildings, Holborn, London EC1N 2QP
Tel: 0870 010 4066 Email: info@ican.org.uk Website: www.ican.org.uk
AFASIC, 2nd Floor, 50–52 Great Sutton Street, London EC1V 0DJ
Tel: 0845 355 5577 (Helpline) Tel: 020 7490 9410 Fax: 020 7251 2834
Email: info@afasic.org.uk Website: www.afasic.org.uk

Tourette's Syndrome (TS)

Tourette's Syndrome (TS) is a neurological disorder characterised by tics. Tics are involuntary rapid or sudden movements or sounds that are frequently repeated. There is a wide range of severity of the condition, with some people having no need to seek medical help while others have a socially disabling condition. The tics can be suppressed for a short time but will be more noticeable when the pupil is anxious or excited.

Main characteristics

Physical tics

Range from simple blinking or nodding through more complex movements to more extreme conditions such as echopraxia (imitating actions seen) or copropraxia (repeatedly making obscene gestures).

Vocal tics

Vocal tics may be as simple as throat-clearing or coughing but can progress to be as extreme as echolalia (the repetition of what was last heard) or coprolalia (the repetition of obscene words).

TS itself causes no behavioural or educational problems, but other, associated disorders such as Attention Deficit Hyperactivity Disorder (ADHD) or Obsessive Compulsive Disorder (OCD) may be present.

How can the RE teacher help?

- Establish a rapport with the pupil.

- Talk to the parents.

- Agree an 'escape route' signal, should the tics become disruptive.

- Allow the pupil to sit at the back of the room to prevent staring.

- Give access to a computer to reduce handwriting.

- Make sure the pupil is not teased or bullied.

- Be alert for signs of anxiety or depression.

Tourette Syndrome (UK) Association, PO Box 26149, Dunfermline, KY12 7YU
Tel: 0845 458 1252 (Helpline)
Tel: 01383 629600 (Admin) Fax: 01383 629609
Email: enquiries@tsa.org.uk Website: www.tsa.org.uk

CHAPTER 4

The Inclusive Religious Education Classroom

Even before a child with special educational needs enters into an RE classroom, there may be structures or traditional ways of doing things which may set that child at a disadvantage. These are not likely to be deliberate obstacles. Quite unconsciously a classroom teacher may have developed particular ways of doing things which can result in some children being limited in the progress they can make. An inclusive RE classroom is one in which the teacher has identified what factors may place a child at a disadvantage and has taken all reasonable steps to remove those disadvantages.

One of the biggest challenges to the teacher of RE in establishing an inclusive classroom is learning to know the children you teach as individuals.

Finding the hidden child

Teachers of RE in mainstream secondary schools often teach large numbers of children. The experience of many teachers of RE is a regular schedule of four or five lessons a day, for five days a week. Each lesson lasting some fifty to seventy minutes, with each class often containing around thirty young people. It is therefore not uncommon for these teachers to be teaching something like 480, or perhaps rising up to 630, children a week. The massive success of the religious education GCSE short course over the last few years has compounded the problem. There are now more young people in Key Stage 4 receiving their entitlement to RE but only in the form of a single weekly lesson. Specialist teachers in Foundation subjects like history or geography may well be teaching similarly large numbers. Nevertheless, it is a fair bet to say that the teacher that sees more faces in their classroom per week than any other teacher in the school, is teaching RE.

Sixteen or more lessons a week, five hundred or more children to be taught, generates in terms of preparation and marking alone an awesome workload. And yet in among all that are individual children. Some of those children are specially gifted and have a real flair for RE, while some of those children have learning difficulties and could be really struggling. Regardless of what can seem like daunting numbers, the inclusive RE classroom has to have at its heart a teacher who knows each one of those children.

Consciously learn names

Some teachers of RE seem to be able to effortlessly learn the names of the children they teach. However, many more have come to realise that to do the job properly they must consciously make an effort to learn names. Any method or combination of methods, as long as they work, are advisable. A seating plan can be helpful, but others deliberately use mnemonics. Others find it helpful to use naming games which require children to identify themselves in the classroom, for example, 'Who am I?'

Who am I?

'Who am I?' involves giving a number of volunteers a 'post-it note' or a label which is attached to their forehead so that the volunteer can't see what is written on the label. On each label is written the name of a famous religious figure, such as Moses, the Pope, the Buddha, Mother Teresa, etc. The volunteer announces their real name and asks, 'Who am I?' The volunteer can ask twenty questions, to which the rest of the class may only answer 'yes' or 'no'. The object of the game is to guess the name on the label before the volunteer runs out of questions.

Other techniques for becoming familiar with names and faces include studying photographs held on school files. Some teachers of RE deliberately take photographs of the children they teach in order to cut and paste the child's photograph onto a piece of display work they have produced. Or a photograph of an entire class is kept in a mark book so that the teacher has a record of names and faces conveniently to hand, but can also learn the names of the children they teach at their leisure.

So much of RE depends on trust and the quality of the relationship between the teacher and the child. The teacher of RE after all is trying to encourage children to talk about their values and to share some of their most deeply held views and judgements. To do this the teacher must be able to demonstrate their genuine respect and interest in the child, and this is lost if the child realises that their name is not being used regularly and often but that they are 'Thingy' or 'Yes, you!'

Actively establish a relationship

Children who have learning difficulties often find that they can avoid embarrassment by becoming invisible. In other words, they don't put their hands up, they avoid answering questions, they don't volunteer information, they don't ask for help and they rarely contribute to class discussions.

In the inclusive classroom the confidence and self-esteem of these children has to be raised if they are to achieve anything like their potential. It is for this reason that some of the most effective teachers of RE do not wear a mask which says, 'We are here to do RE business only.' They seek instead to actively establish a relationship by acknowledging children by name and saying hello outside of the classroom. They ask children about their interests and their lives and remember what they talked about. They might share a joke, accept a crisp, remember their birthday. They give gifts like a press cutting or a postcard which they hand to the child, saying, 'I saw this and thought of you.' Effective teachers of RE acknowledge that children live lives outside of school, and they attempt to build up a picture of the whole child. Often classroom teachers report that their success comes from the relationship they have established with children because they got involved in running the basketball team, or set up a drama club, or because they participate in geography field trips. As RE is about exploring children's inner space as well as the world of religions out there, any young person, whether they are a gifted learner or one who finds learning hard work, will respond better to a teacher who they feel knows and cares about them.

Although it might be interesting to be taught RE for a couple of days by a Robocop or a Vulcan, they are not likely to have much long-term success.

The learning environment

If RE is being taught largely in a specific classroom, most teachers will want to customise that room in various ways. Many teachers of RE will fill display boards with a mix of visual and written material. Some of this material will be commercially available and some of it may be examples of children's work both written and graphic. Key words and religious artefacts may also be added.

This is all very well. Sometimes the effect can be very appealing, but all too often this is not the case. It is well worthwhile looking with a more critical eye at the display and asking, 'How can this environment be enhanced in order to support learning?' All too often in an attempt not to be biased, a little bit about all religions is found around the walls. From an adult's point of view this is understandable, but from the point of view of a young person with learning difficulties the effect can be confusing. Far from enhancing learning, the classroom environment presents a jumbled mass of data. In some classrooms pupils are attempting to work in a space which is a source of both mental as well as sensory overload.

Wheelchair users and visual impairment

Thought also needs to be given to the height and font size of any material which is displayed. Children who are wheelchair users simply will not be able to see display material which is set much above the level of their head. A large amount of commercially available RE display material often has text information which is little more than 12 to 16 points. For a child sitting ten feet away, print of this size is impossible to decipher. For a child with a visual impairment, no matter how closely they scrutinise such information, they remain excluded from a significant part of its content. Customising posters and graphic material with captions printed in a much larger font can help turn what would otherwise be little more than wall cover into an effective educational resource.

Display boards need not only be a visual experience but may also be tactile or even a multi-sensory experience appealing to touch, smell and hearing. Artefacts, like Islamic prayer beads, various types of crosses, Buddhist prayer wheels, Hindu kum kum powder, a Challah loaf, a Shofar (Ram's horn), a Salvation Army tambourine or a Kenyan church drum, can all, with the discreet use of fishing tackle, be safely attached to display boards.

Implicit religious material

There is also plenty of material from the natural world which raises important religious questions. A display of leaves not only provides a tactile opportunity for children with a visual impairment, but may be used to reflect on the appearance of design in the natural world and how such intricate design may have come about. Forms of life in a dormant stage, like grass seed, an acorn, tulip bulbs, or a coconut, might be put on display to be touched and smelt, along with, if possible, examples of more vigorous stages of their life cycle. By doing this, questions may be raised about the origin and transitions of life. Questions may be asked about human life and whether we also perhaps transcend out of this life into another form of existence, the like of which we can only guess at.

Children with special needs often confuse one religion with another. One way of helping children with this problem is by separating information about the different religions using space and colour. One section of the classroom may be colour-coded using purple frieze paper, and this area alone is used for displaying material about Christianity. Another section of the classroom may be colour-coded with green frieze paper and this area alone is used for Islam. Red may be used to colour-code Hinduism. Pale blue may be used for Judaism.

If it is the case that the class is exploring how two religions can be similar or distinctively different, the point can be reinforced through display; but do so by creating a separate display which is separately zoned. For example, children's awareness that what Muslims believe about the Prophet Muhammad is not the same as what Christians claim about Jesus may be supported in a separately zoned space. If this point appears as a display but is jumbled in among other data about Islam, it is hardly surprising that young people with learning difficulties don't get the point and are left simply confused.

The RE classroom should not bombard young people with masses of data, ideas and information and leave them to absorb it and sort it out. The teacher of RE should help young people to develop a mental construct of what a religion is about. This is done by providing children with a manageable number of key ideas or beliefs set in the context of a particular religion. These key ideas may be displayed in a classroom with the fundamental points indicated that are to be learnt at this stage. This material may be presented in a large font which the pupils can read from anywhere in the classroom. By doing so key messages about a religion can be pressed home and reinforced in order to establish confident and secure learning.

Let's look at an example of this in practice. During a series of lessons about the Jewish Sabbath, the Shabbat, the children might be asked to suggest not only what Jews do on the Sabbath but why the day is so important. There are many answers to that question. The Sabbath is important because:

- keeping the Sabbath is a requirement in the Torah

- the Sabbath recalls events associated with the exodus

- it is a reminder of the story of God's creation

- it is an ancient Jewish tradition

- it provides a regular welcome break from the routine of life.

Given the complex and subtle nature of religion, all of these answers are true. As the question is being explored, one boy whose reading and writing skills are very limited but who has a flair for a vivid metaphor suggests, 'It's the glue that keeps them together.'

This is a moment of serendipity in the RE classroom. The classroom display might well show a large poster of a Jewish family celebrating the Sabbath. It may well have information about the candles, the bread, the wine, but in 350mm font are the words, 'It's the glue that keeps them together.' There is no pretence that this is a full or complete answer. What it does do, however, is provide a clear and manageable piece of learning which children can retain. It affirms the self-esteem of a child. It sends a message to the pupils that their ideas will be recognised and that their contributions are not a sideshow to a more correct expert view. All the other legitimate answers are not being ignored. All that is happening is that the classroom teacher is managing the classroom environment by focusing on a key idea in order to ensure that children learn and are not simply confused.

For some students avoiding confusing them with too much information is particularly necessary. For example, for children that have an autistic spectrum disorder (ASD), although visual clues are important, it is just as important to avoid a visual data overload. Visual distractions and smells may unsettle a student. In some cases a visual barrier or even a study carrel may be necessary in order to enable pupils to cope more effectively with their hyper-sensitivity.

The value of using material drawn from the natural world has already been referred to. Powerful visual images like a sunrise, or a magnified snowflake, a view of earth from space, accompanied by questions like, 'Is there a super-intelligent being who created this?' 'Are there signs of God in the universe?' 'What are we doing here?' serve as reminders of central issues in religious education. Newspaper cuttings about events like floods or earthquakes, or news items which raise ethical issues like crime, medical procedures or scientific research, all help to make it clear that religion is relevant and contemporary.

Example

The *Daily Mail*, 13 February 2004, reported that South Korean doctors were 'Playing God' and had 'breached one of the greatest ethical boundaries'. Is the cloning of human cells for seven days 'playing God'?

Large and prominent messages, for example 30 cm-high letters spelling out the word THINK, can provide a permanent reminder to pupils that there is an expectation that they should voice their own ideas. A giant ear with the word LISTEN printed underneath reinforces the message that RE discussion isn't about scoring points but is about listening to what others have to say and taking this into account as pupils form their view.

In order to help children to learn in RE it is helpful to provide permanent reminders of the aims of the subject. The tendency for some children, even though the point may have been made clear earlier, is to lapse into thinking RE is about encouraging faith and attempting to nurture them into a faith commitment. The teacher of RE needs to create a learning environment which makes it clear that RE is about exploring, understanding, asking and thinking and is not about violating their right to their views. Similar support can be given to pupils' understanding of the subject and their awareness of what they are being asked to do in order to move forward, by displaying pupil-friendly levels of attainment. Many of these are based on the levels published in *The Non-Statutory National Framework* and are increasingly being found in local authorities' agreed syllabuses.

Wall of Wisdom

A Wall of Wisdom is an identified space in the classroom on which a record is kept of some of the more startling and thoughtful comments made by the children. Young people often come up with remarkable and fascinating statements. Sometimes as part of a discussion, or as a response to something that has happened to them, or maybe seemingly out of nowhere, children can say things which raise a difficult question or bring a fresh insight. Not unlike the brazen comment of the child in the story of 'The Emperor's New Clothes', children say things like:

'Why are some people so 'orrible – I don't think they mean to be?'

'God is everywhere like the air you breathe.'

'Life is like a long journey.'

'If God made the world, who made God?'

'Why do some religious people hate other people?'

'The best time to pray is when it is quiet and you need God.'

'People are scared of what they don't know.'

'Why did my Gran have to die when we all loved her?'

Instead of these statements being lost forever, the teacher records them onto large speech bubbles which are then displayed on the Wall of Wisdom. The name of the child, their class and the date is also recorded on the bubble. If they have no objection the speech bubble can be further personalised by adding a photograph of the child.

Umair points to his question on the Wall of Wisdom.

See: RE Today *16/3 (Summer 1999).*

As the comments on the Wall come from the children, it can be particularly rewarding for young people who have reading and writing difficulties to find themselves being listened to and affirmed in this way. Also it provides a message to young people that RE isn't just about organised religion or what grown-ups think. RE is also about them, their experiences of the world and how they respond to life.

Classroom layout

Seating arrangements for RE classrooms has been a subject of discussion for many years. As well as the obvious requirements, like making sure that there is enough space for all pupils, including wheelchair users, and support staff to sit and move about, there is certainly a lot to be said for giving serious thought to how seating affects the social dynamics of a classroom and how it supports some activities and limits others. In the influential book *New Methods in RE Teaching* by John Hammond, David Hay, Joy Moxon *et al.* (1990), the experience of teachers that make widespread use of kinaesthetic experiential activities and discussion circle time was that traditional rows of desks confined teachers and pupils. These teachers' classroom furniture was rearranged with tables lining the outside walls. Chairs were arranged to face outwards for written work, but could easily be turned inwards, making a horseshoe or circle, for discussion.

Not all teachers will find it practical to arrange their RE classroom in this way and not all teachers, even if they could, would feel comfortable with this layout.

Nevertheless, having children seated behind desks facing towards the teacher signals that the teacher is the dominant voice in the classroom and that children's comments are to be largely directed through the teacher. Genuine class discussion which involves pupil-to-pupil exchanges, not just pupil-to-teacher exchanges, is extremely difficult for most children unless they can face each other and see each other's reactions as is possible when sitting in a circle. Even if the setup isn't permanent, the mark of an inclusive RE classroom is flexibility, so that pupils can relatively easily form a discussion circle.

Group work

Flexibility is also needed in the RE classroom so that group work can regularly take place. Groups enable pupils to learn from each other, try out ideas and gain confidence. They provide pupils with opportunities to learn to co-operate and work together as a team. Friendship groups are an obvious arrangement; however, this should not be the only arrangement in the RE classroom. Putting pupils together who don't normally relate well reinforces important RE aims. A central part of RE is recognising our differences and respecting diversity. Children shouldn't just theoretically talk about this. They should have opportunities to try it out and experience it for themselves in the relatively safe environment of the classroom.

This can be planned by the teacher, or on some occasions children may be randomly paired in order to encourage young people to interact with others in the classroom with whom they hardly socialise. Games like, 'Find your partner', which involves the pupils randomly picking a paper on which is written a well known character or person, e.g. David Beckham, Posh Spice, Harry Potter, Ron Weasley, generates a sense of fun in the classroom and can help combat any sense of nervousness or tension. (See the CD for notes on turn-taking. Where pupils find it difficult to wait for their turn, try the circle-time approach of passing round an object – only the person holding the object can speak.)

Literacy skills

The teacher of RE will often find in their classroom a wide diversity of literacy skills. Some pupils may be very skilful readers and writers, while others may have real difficulty, resulting in 'writing apprehension', avoidance strategies and a cycle of failure. The approach of some teachers is to follow a line of least resistance. Writing activities are kept to a minimum, and where they are used they tend to be very simplistic. Composition is largely avoided, and instead pupils' writing is largely limited to lists, labels, bullet-pointed notes, word searches, single word answers or cloze activities.

Although speaking and listening skills are very important, so also are the skills of reading and writing, and the RE classroom has an important role in helping children to gain more confidence and raise their level of achievement. To do that, teachers of RE need to do more than set writing tasks for children and be enthusiastic. Writing is the most demanding of all language skills. Pupils have difficulty not only with the mechanical aspects of writing, like handwriting, spelling and punctuation. They may also have a problem with composition, or having something to say, and find it difficult to plan, sequence ideas, edit and revise their work.

To help young people make progress, the following are some suggestions.

- *Demonstrate the writing process* – this involves the teacher modelling the process of composition. The teacher provides a commentary on how ideas may be organised and how early stages from talk, to notes, to eventually formal writing, may take place.

- *Shared composition* – this involves the pupils themselves largely undertaking the composition and the editing process, with the teacher serving as a scribe.

- *Supported writing* – the pupils work on a writing task but with supportive strategies, like a writing partner or a writing frame. (See p.56 for example.)

- *Diagnostic support* – some children that have difficulty with writing do so partly because they have a particular recurring weakness. For example, some children use long rambling sentences with repetitive use of conjunctions . . . 'and then they pray and then they hear the Bible and then they all stand up . . .'. Or some children repeatedly misspell the same words, e.g. 'beleve', 'Jewes', 'becuse'. Such difficulties need to be homed in on and children actively supported so that the problem can be overcome. (See Appendix 3 for notes on spelling.)

- *Prepare for writing* – help pupils to generate ideas and record them by preliminarily discussion, brainstorming, mind-mapping, visualising, and identifying analogies, metaphors and key words.

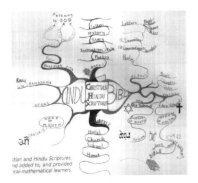

- *Make writing exciting* – often writing activities in RE are rather formal, if not dull; for example, 'Describe what is said and done at an infant baptism.' Try to pep up the activity and give children a motive for writing by introducing a setting, an audience, a novelty, a

Mind Mapping. See: RE Today 20/3 *(Summer 2003).*

source of amusement: 'Xyglubb, a cultural observer from a distant galaxy observes an infant baptism. He has decided to send an intergalactic fax to his home planet. It begins, "I've discovered that these disgusting earthlings try to drown their children. In a ghastly ceremony . . ." Help Xyglubb write the fax so that he doesn't get into trouble.'

- *Drafting and redrafting* – few people can produce a sustained piece of fluent writing in a single draft. Give pupils an opportunity to learn from their first effort and return to the task in order to improve the work and polish their own writing. Word processing can be of great help to pupils in this process, as it enables pupils to redraft a work many times, eventually ending up with a product they can take pride in, and perhaps in some form have published.

The main beliefs Muslims have about God are that . . .

Muslims also believe that God is . . .

Christians and Muslims have similar views about God, as in both religions they believe . . .

However, Muslims do not believe . . .

My own view about God is that . . .

(There are more writing frames on the accompanying CD)

CHAPTER 5

Teaching and Learning Styles

Our knowledge of how children learn and what normally are the characteristics of effective teaching have improved dramatically over the last few decades. Just like any other subject, RE lessons benefit from having a snappy start which engages the pupils. Being clear about the aim of the lesson and sharing that aim with the pupils can also greatly help. When identifying an aim it is usually better to avoid a statement which is very unspecific. Telling young people that the aim of the lesson is to deepen their understanding of the Bible can only result in uncertainty as to whether that aim has been achieved. Whereas if the aim can be specified in a clearer form, for example, 'By the end of the lesson you will know three reasons why the Bible is believed to be a holy book', pupils can leave a lesson with a clearer sense of achievement knowing that they have gained something.

Plenaries are also an important weapon in the RE teacher's arsenal. They make it possible for pupils to demonstrate and reinforce what they have learnt. However, it is important that plenaries should involve the pupils and that they don't simply become an opportunity for the teacher to tell the pupils what they have been taught.

There can be few people today, who are involved in education, who are not aware of Howard Gardner's ideas about multiple intelligence. Using his ideas in their simplest form we know some young people in our classrooms are mainly visual learners, others are mainly auditory while others are mainly kinaesthetic learners. In order to establish an inclusive classroom the teacher of RE must respond to the learning strengths of different children and try and accommodate their different needs.

Visual learners

Most people find that learning something is easier if a picture is provided. For large numbers of young people with learning difficulties a diet largely of words, whether spoken or written, unsupported by visual material, seriously limits their ability to learn. However, a great amount of religious material is available to us visually. The following are just some examples of how to make effective use of visual material.

Deciphering visual information

Avoid being over-didactic, by providing an explanation or commentary on visual material provided. Instead, help the pupils to develop their visual and oral skills by giving them opportunities to decipher information for themselves. For example, provide pupils with a photograph, perhaps of an infant baptism or a Muslim at prayer. Give the pupils several minutes looking and thinking time and invite the pupils to report back what they can see in the photograph.

Suggest motive and purpose

Children with learning difficulties don't want to be patronised with tasks which are too easy. To create more challenge, pupils might be asked to suggest what cannot be seen, that is, motive, purpose and feelings. Children should be given several minutes to look and think before they answer. Questions should be phrased without fussy elaboration; for example, 'Look at the photo – why do you think this man is doing this?' The teacher should try to avoid suggesting in their tone or manner that there is a single correct answer or that they know the answer and that the child has to somehow guess what the teacher is thinking.

Storyboarding

Children with learning difficulties can find it easier to recall the details of a story using visual memory based on storyboarding. Teachers of RE do need to avoid becoming too preoccupied, or bogged down, with the accuracy with which children can recall a religious story. Religious stories like the Easter story, the Genesis creation story, or the Sikh Baisakhi story, are important. However, being able to accurately recall them is of secondary importance compared with having an insight into what the story may be telling us or how it may inform our own lives. It can happen that children will repeatedly stumble over the details of a story. Nevertheless, simply because they cannot get the recall right does not mean that children should not be given an opportunity to respond to a story. A child that may find it difficult to articulate the details of a story may well have a sufficiently effective grasp of the story so that they can talk about what the story means.

Religious art

Visual images are not just neutral records of reality. This is particularly true of religious art. Pupils should be encouraged to look at religious art and ask, 'What is the artist trying to tell me?' 'What are the beliefs of the artist?' Children who may have difficulty with reading and writing can often show a shrewd ability to read an image.

In order to create an opportunity for pupils to do this, it is important to avoid the temptation to tell pupils what an image means. By giving pupils looking and thinking time they will perceive answers which will stay with them long after they have forgotten anything that the teacher might have said.

Comparing religious art

The claim that artists have beliefs and attitudes which are reflected in the art they produce can be made even clearer by comparing the work of two pieces of art. Particularly in Christian art, over the centuries, certain themes have been tackled by many artists. This makes it possible to directly compare the views represented in two works of art. This can be achieved by displaying two works of art like Grunewald's *Crucifixion* and Raphael's *Crucifixion* and asking of each painting, 'What does this painting tell you?' By using a visual strategy in this way young people can find it easier to learn and discuss new ideas and yet avoid being confronted with a daunting page of text.

Implicit religious images

Many children have little experience of organised religion and view any organised authority as an irrelevance which does not understand or address their needs. And yet many of these young people are working on issues going on inside them which are of a profoundly religious nature. It is for this reason that when given the opportunity to pause and wonder at visual material like a rural landscape, moonlight on water, or a close-up of a dandelion, young people can astonish us with the quality of the questions these images pose for them.

As well as images of the natural world, images which remind us of the world we live in can be equally stimulating. Some of the images may reflect pain and grief in the world; for example, a village destroyed by an earthquake, a victim of a brutal crime, or the mushroom cloud of a hydrogen bomb. Some images have a message of hope and joy; for example, the loving care of a trained nurse, the companionship and joy in the faces of an elderly married couple or the laughter of street children playing in a slum.

Objects and artefacts

Images which raise questions and stimulate healthy discussion do not have to be two-dimensional. Arranging the pupils into a circle and placing into the centre of the circle a single object like an acorn, an expensive bottle of cosmetic, a vase of decaying flowers, a Big Mac, a pair of designer label trainers, can all serve as a stimulus to lively discussion. Pupils who sometimes hardly ever speak are suddenly revealed as informed students of globalisation, the power of the media, materialism, spirituality and happiness, death and decay. A religious artefact can similarly be used as a stimulus. A quality artefact, for example a Shiva Nata-raja, a crucifix, or an image of a laughing Buddha, can provide the prompt for a discussion on what God is like, the purpose of prayer, the role of sacrifice and the meaning of salvation.

Controlled disclosure

It is important to try and add a sense of drama to the experience of first seeing an artefact. In RE this is commonly called 'controlled disclosure'. The object should be covered and so cannot be seen as the pupils take their seats. When the pupils are ready and their attention is focused the cover is removed, and the experience begins. Sometimes the disclosing of the object is made even more partial by removing only part of the cover, or by allowing the students a partial experience of the artefact by being allowed to touch it underneath the cover but not see it. The point of this is that the disclosure should not be casual but should have a sense of occasion about it. It is also important to present a religious artefact as far as is possible with a sense of quality and respect. After all, a religious artefact may often embody some of the most deeply felt convictions a human may have. To achieve this sense of respect it is desirable to make use of signals, and a quality stand, a tablecloth or a coloured velvet cover is often used. Children with learning difficulties are often very sensitive to these signals. Certainly a religious artefact must not be presented in any way which could be perceived as being casual, sloppy or tatty.

A single stimulus

The power of the strategy is not increased by using more and more images or artefacts. Showing young people many images of poverty can turn children off, making them immune and thereby impoverishing rather than heightening the experience. Showing many images or artefacts related to prayer may confuse the issue and raise too many questions. A single stimulus, like a well-presented image or artefact which the pupils are given plenty of time to reflect on, can have a much more powerful impact.

Films and video

As well as the still image, it is not possible to ignore the value of the moving image in the inclusive RE classroom. Using usually the video it is possible to show pupils Muslims undertaking the Hajj, Christians receiving holy communion and Jews celebrating the Passover. Using child-friendly cartoon characters, Christian, Sikh and Hindu stories can be shown to young people with little more effort than pressing the 'play' button.

Given all this material, one would think the teacher of RE could hardly fail in the classroom. However, the video is not a passport to RE Shangri-La. Often RE video material is visually decidedly uninteresting for young people. A great deal of religious video material rarely has any lavish special effects, the pace is often drawn out and the language is often little more than a descriptive commentary.

For this reason it is often inappropriate to play the whole 20 or 30 minutes of an RE video. Instead, a four- or five-minute video clip may well result in a much more effective learning outcome. Video material often carries several different messages, so it can help if young people are invited to focus on one specific task prior to viewing. For example, pupils might be told that after the video clip they are to work with a partner and come up with three reasons why a Muslim might be unhappy if they had never undertaken a pilgrimage to Mecca in their life.

Video can be turned into a far less passive medium if young people are entrusted with a camcorder and invited to make their own video. Some teachers have had tremendous success with young people who have found it very difficult to learn in the classroom but have recorded thoughtful comments on camera reflecting on what it is like, for example, to be a young Muslim growing up in Britain.

Contemporary film

Contemporary film can often provide rich material which the teacher of RE can make use of. Some films have a fairly obvious religious theme, for example Richard Attenborough's *Gandhi*, Franco Zeffirelli's *Jesus of Nazareth*, or Moustapha Akkad's *The Message*. But sometimes films draw upon and explore spiritual and religious themes in a far less explicit way. Judicious use of this material can help students recognise in popular youth culture a depth which they have sensed themselves but may not have fully recognised. *The Matrix*, for example, raises issues about the power of illusion, the struggle to understand the difference between reality and appearance and the concept of a saviour. *Star Wars* and *Lord of the Rings* present spectacular accounts of good against evil set in the form of classic dualism. *Terminator 2* has some very interesting comments on the sanctity of life, the difference between man and machine, sacrifice and salvation. *Toy Story* has a lot to say about rivalry, fear of the newcomer, loyalty and courage.

Soaps and series

It is well known that TV soaps have over the years featured major storylines on moral and social issues, like euthanasia, adultery, domestic violence, racism and abortion. However, it is also true that a number of cult TV series have survived because they also contain a great deal of thoughtful writing. *Star Trek*, for example, often with subtlety, explores themes like living with diversity, what it means to be human, how under stress the human spirit can grow, and the aspiration to strive and make more of oneself. *The Simpsons* in among the jokes has all sorts of references to religion and theology, like Bart selling his soul, Homer breaking the eighth commandment and Lisa as the voice of Christian social awareness.

This material opens up real possibilities for young people who in the RE classroom have learning difficulties. Young people who may have very little to say about Divali or Confirmation, given the opportunity may have a great deal to say of a religious nature about a film or a TV programme they know well and feel passionate about.

Auditory learners

Some people have a particularly strong response to sound. They find that their ability to learn is much improved if the learning environment is aurally enriched.

Religious music

The strong association between music and particular religions can be used to establish a memorable theme. So, for example, as the pupils enter a classroom have playing 'To Life' from *Fiddler on the Roof*. This can set the theme of the lesson, which is about the gusty joy, and exuberant way in which many Jewish festivals like Purim and Simchat Torah are celebrated. The sound of the harmonium and tabla may be used to mark the beginning of a lesson about Sikh worship.

We know that our minds are alerted and that we pay much more attention if things happen out of the ordinary. The more we can make lessons exceptional or different and take children by surprise, for example, with the shock of The London Community Gospel Choir ringing in their ears, the greater are the chances that learning will take place.

Mood music

Music may also be used which has no particular religious associations, but it may set the appropriate mood in order to reinforce the lesson. For example, a group of pupils report to the whole class the story of Dietrich Bonhoeffer and his resistance to the Nazis. As they do so Carl Davis's theme 'The World at War' is played in the background. As the pupils tell the story, there is an intensity in the classroom which, had there been no music, would have been absent.

Contemporary music

Contemporary rock and pop music is very important in the lives of many young people. Although much of it may have little substance, some of the best provides a genuine mini-commentary on serious issues which morally, spiritually and religiously are highly relevant. For example, Pink in *Family Portrait* assumes the voice of a young girl experiencing the break-up of her parents' marriage. Shania Twain in *Ka-ching* mocks a world which makes a religion of having commodities. Black Eyed Peas in *Where is the Love?* deplores negative images which contaminate the minds of young people and asks what has happened to the values of humanity?

The potential of this material in the RE classroom for drawing young people into thought and discussion is immense. However, using contemporary music in RE is fraught with danger and has to be handled carefully. It is important that the teacher doesn't come across as false, attempting to exploit the popularity of youth culture.

Combining music with images

Contemporary music can be very effectively combined with visual images which can provide a springboard to reflection and discussion. Young people perhaps working with a partner could be invited to select a piece of music which they feel has something significant to say. Their task is to combine the music with some still images. Before beginning the task a discussion with the pupils takes place so that there is agreement about the sort of messages and values that would be appropriate. After the teacher has had a chance to preview the work the finished product could be shown to the other pupils. The possibilities of drawing upon young people's strengths using ICT with this sort of assignment are clear.

Reflection time

RE has an important role in educating young people's emotions and feelings. One important way of achieving this is by building in reflection time. For example: in a lesson about Martin Luther King, using improvised drama, the pupils explore situations involving racism. In the discussion following, a pupil describes their own recent experience of racism. There is a genuine sense of outrage at the injustice. The teacher suggests that they should have time for reflection. A candle is lit and the teacher invites the pupils to think about what it is like to be the victim of racism and what they can do to stop racism. There is silence in the room for over a minute. Following the reflection time the teacher invites pupils to share, if they wish, what thoughts they had while they were reflecting. A number of the pupils describe their feelings about racism and suggest ways of combating it.

However, reflection time cannot just be inserted into an RE lesson at any arbitrary point. The teacher has to plan a lesson so that the reflection time is appropriate.

Reflection time and music

It is however true that some young people find it difficult to cope with silence. For those pupils who are initially restless this usually disappears over a short period of time as they get used to the experience. Reflection time can be supported by the use of music. Reflection music is usually slow and restful. Music which has a mystical quality can be particularly helpful as found in the pan flute music of Gheorghe Zamfir, or in pieces like Erik Satie's *Gymnopedies*.

Guided fantasy

Another way of supporting reflection time is by the use of guided fantasy. Guided fantasy is when the teacher, usually working from a prepared script, invites the pupils to imagine situations in which reflection or relaxation may be made easier. The teacher may begin by saying, for example, 'Imagine you are leaving the classroom. It is a hot, sunny day. You are walking down a country lane and then you find yourself in a meadow . . .' As with the reflection time, guided fantasy can also be supported by music.

Special effects

Although it is not specific to RE, there are certain sound-effects and special clips of music the novelty of which has widespread appeal for young people and supports their learning. The ticking clock sound-effect from the TV programme *Countdown* can be played to mark the end of time available to pupils to complete a particular activity. There are plenty of other special sound-effects which alert pupils, generate interest, give lessons a touch of humour and make lessons more memorable; for example, *Mission Impossible* might accompany the story of Jackie Pullinger, and *Thus Spake Zarathustra* could herald a presentation on Creation.

Religious sounds

Just as there are certain three-dimensional religious artefacts, so there are also certain sounds which are associated with particular religious traditions. Examples of these include the sound of the Jewish Shofar or ram's horn, the Islamic call to prayer and Buddhist chanting. These sounds obviously do have a place in the RE classroom. However, as with three-dimensional artefacts, so also these sound artefacts have to be handled with care. The Islamic call to prayer, the adhan, for example, may have a haunting beauty when heard over the rooftops of Ankara. But the sound of a recording played through two 2-watt speakers can be very disappointing. If good recordings of such sounds cannot be found, a short discussion may be necessary so that pupils don't end up making inappropriate judgements.

Kinaesthetic learners

In education we have become increasingly aware that asking children to stand up and do things is by far the most effective way in which large numbers of pupils can learn. The following are some examples of kinaesthetic strategies which can be applied in the RE classroom.

Religious artefacts

Bringing physical objects like a Qur'an, a chalice, a menorah, into the classroom makes a religion much more real to young people. Appropriate respect has to be accorded to these objects in their presentation and handling. Pupils can gain a much more memorable encounter if they are permitted to have a hands-on experience. The appropriate handling of religious artefacts, picking up the signals from the teacher, is part of the lesson in respect which these objects make possible.

Providing a contrast

One way of varying the experience and of highlighting the special features of an artefact is by contrasting a religious artefact with a non-religious object.

Pupils might, for example, be invited to identify the difference between the uncomfortable, prickly feel of a coconut doormat compared with the soft, velvety, feel of a Muslim prayer mat. The contrasting difference in the colour and decoration might also be noted.

Simulation or mock ritual

Religious ceremonies and festivals like infant baptism, the Passover meal, Arti and Amrit, particularly lend themselves to simulation. It is important to make it clear that what is taking place is not a real baptism or a real arti. Real religious ceremonies and rituals involve the inner intentions and beliefs of the participants. A simulation is an attempt to reconstruct the external movements and words of a religious ritual. Only volunteers should be asked to take part, and

frequently it is well worthwhile the teacher freezing the action and reminding all present that what is happening is not a real religious ceremony but a simulation. Special touches which can add to the reality of the simulation are well worthwhile. So a simulated Passover meal is much more memorable if the pupils get to eat some genuine matzah (unleavened bread) and some prepared haroset.

The visit

As an opportunity for an experience which provides pupils with a lasting memory, the RE visit has few rivals. Although it involves a large investment of time, the rewards can be tremendous. The great majority of RE visits are to places of worship – for example, churches, mosques, gurdwaras – but other possibilities include exhibitions like the Beth Shalom Holocaust Centre, the IPCI Exhibition on Islam and the Anne Frank Exhibition.

Visits often have an unexpected educational bonus. Young people, for example, are often impressed by the generosity of members of the Sikh community or the friendliness they experience in the mosque. Visits often remove the sense of wariness and distrust. They often result in improved relationships between teachers and pupils as the pupils are conscious that the teacher has made an effort on their behalf.

Although there are usually spin-off benefits to visits, it is still advisable to plan the visit so that there is an aim involving clear learning. Establishing a good first-hand contact with the member of the faith community that will greet your party and show them around can be of great help. A visit is usually of much more benefit if the pupils are given clear opportunities to meet members of the faith community, focus on significant features of the building and have a chance to ask questions which have been considered prior to the visit. Children with learning difficulties can often be helped to get something extra out of a visit by giving them a special task or activity. For example, they might be given charge of a digital camera or a single flash camera to make a photographic record of their visit. Or using a minidisc recorder they may make an audio diary of their visit.

The natural world

A very valuable resource for the teacher of RE is the natural world outside the classroom. Children can learn a great deal through activities like 'Hoop', 'Trust walk' or 'Sounds'. 'Hoop' involves taking pupils to a field or patch of grass on a dry day. The pupils put a hoop on the ground and spend some time carefully looking at what can be seen inside the hoop. After a while the pupils come together and share their discoveries and thoughts. 'Trustwalk' has the pupils working together in pairs. One pupil is the leader and the other pupil is blindfolded. In a natural area the leader guides their partner visiting smells, shapes and textures. 'Sounds' involves having the pupils lie down on their backs with both fists held up in the air. Whenever they hear a sound, it may be a leaf falling, the wind in the trees or a bird singing, the pupil lifts a finger. After a while the pupils are invited to reflect and then talk about the experience.

Activities like these may be criticised because they provide little in the way of overt learning about religion. This would be a fair criticism if the pupils were only invited to stare at a patch of grass for a while and nothing else. The reflection and sharing of responses is essential. The purpose of these activities is to bring young people closer to the original experiences which probably gave rise to religious impulses in the first place. By doing so pupils may gain a much greater understanding of the questions and feelings which form the basis of religious faith.

'Human graph'

'Human graph' enables self-conscious adolescents to have their view on an issue expressed without having to reveal their own position. Pupils are invited to think about an issue, such as 'Does prayer really work?' After some thinking time the pupils record their attitude by choosing a number 1 to 5 which they write on a piece of paper. Number 1 represents the view that there is a very low chance that prayer works. Number 5 represents the view that there is a very high chance. The paper with the number on it is left unsigned and placed into a box. After the papers have been jumbled up, each pupil removes a paper from the box. Numbers 1 to 5 are placed onto the floor. The pupils are invited to form a human bar chart by standing in line by the number on the floor which corresponds to the number they picked out of the box. Seeing how the views of the class vary, the pupils might be invited to suggest reasons why people hold different views on this issue. Or in some cases pupils, realising they are not alone in their views, feel encouraged to talk about their beliefs.

'Human continuum'

'Human continuum' involves inviting the pupils to imagine a line in the classroom. One end of the line represents a point of view. The other end represents the opposite point of view. The space between the two ends represents the various shades of grey. Following discussion on a controversial issue, for example 'Has religion been more responsible for peace than war?' pupils are asked to stand in the space on the continuum line which most accurately represents their view.

Pupils are often surprised by the position taken up by fellow classmates, and this can prompt deeper discussion. Another advantage of the technique for the inclusive classroom is that it enables all pupils to say where they stand on an issue even though articulating their view neatly into words might be difficult for them.

Role-play

There are a whole range of educational drama techniques like 'hot-seating', 'freeze frame', or 'robe of the expert' which lend themselves to adaptation in the RE classroom. Role-play usually involves improvised drama. Two or three pupils are given a role and a scenario and are invited to role-play what might be said or done. For example, a scenario might be: In a school where most children are Christian or nominally Christian, Sikh pupils are being mocked for wearing the turban. Role 1 – Kimberley thinks what is going on is a harmless bit of fun and that Sikhs in the school shouldn't be so sensitive. Role 2 – Darren thinks that all Christians have a responsibility to stop racial and religious intolerance wherever they see it. Role-play a scene between Kimberley and Darren.

The role-play may be extended with additional pupils, in role, being invited to join the conversation. For example, Role 3 – Lisa thinks all signs of religious commitment should be banned in a school. For successful improvised role-play pupils do need to have some thinking and preparation time. They should also be given an opportunity to step out of role and talk about how they felt about the role.

Mime

Some children when asked to describe a baptism or how Muslims worship shrug their shoulders or look blank, apparently in complete ignorance of such rituals. In some cases such a response does not mean that they do not have any knowledge of such rituals. Mime can help children show that they have a body memory of rituals, ceremonies and festivals which is not easily available to them in language. The pupils are given some planning or research time. They then mime the ritual. The rest of the pupils, perhaps provided with a list of choices, guess what ritual is being mimed.

CHAPTER 6

Monitoring and Assessment

Ofsted reports that in RE, assessment is a particular weakness. The 2002/3 Ofsted report on RE in secondary schools says that, 'In spite of improvements, weaknesses identified in previous years persist including assessment in a quarter of schools . . .' The report goes on to say that there remain inadequacies in day-to-day assessment in the classroom and also weaknesses in the 'use of assessment to guide curricular planning and provide for the varying needs of pupils . . .' (Ofsted 2004).

Why is assessment in RE a particular weakness?

There are many reasons why assessment in RE is generally poor. Part of the problem has been due to poor or unclear ideas, which have found their way into some local agreed syllabuses. Another difficulty has been the low priority that has been given to assessment while other issues – like meeting statutory requirements, introducing relevant schemes of work, developing effective teaching strategies and improving resources – have been seen as more urgent.

A further difficulty has been a certain scepticism, sometimes found in religious education, towards assessment. There are obvious aspects of the subject like the development of factual knowledge which lend themselves to assessment. For example, it is not too difficult to devise ways of assessing whether or not a child knows the names of certain sacred books, or can identify the key features of a church, or can recognise certain religious artefacts. The acquisition of factual knowledge is clearly a necessary part of RE. However, acquiring factual knowledge has always been regarded as less important in RE compared with much more significant aims. RE is not about merely naming and labelling. The teaching of RE involves something much deeper, and the suspicion of many involved in RE has been that the most significant aspects of the subject could not be assessed. This resulted in the belief that if RE followed other subjects down the path of assessment, the subject would be in danger of becoming a parody of its true self. Teachers of RE would only teach what could be measured or assessed to the neglect of the more nebulous but much more worthwhile aspects of the subject.

Indeed, it has been suggested that not only the most significant aspects of RE could not be assessed, but that in some areas assessment would be inappropriate and should not be attempted. To do so it is claimed involved a sort of intrusion, particularly into the private life of the child. The suggestion is that the attempt to assess some areas would be inappropriate as it might involve assessing a pupil's own beliefs and values. By doing so teachers would be judging pupils to be 'right' or 'wrong' in their beliefs. Clearly this would be wrong. Teachers have no authority to impose their own judgements on the beliefs of others. To do so would be a failure to engage in an educational process, but instead to undertake a confessional, or perhaps even a propaganda-like activity, which conflicts with the aims of RE.

Much of this scepticism and reluctance to develop assessment in RE has been due to confused thinking. However, in the last decade or so there has been an increasing realisation that RE cannot continue to be so reticent about assessment. The overwhelming evidence available today tells us that formative assessment helps young people to learn. Indeed assessment for learning is crucial. One of the main reasons why some children become bored and fed up in their RE lessons and fail to learn is because they do not properly know what is being asked of them or what they need to do to get better. Effective teaching of RE, like any other curriculum area, must be interactive. In the RE classroom teachers need to know their pupils' strengths and weaknesses. They need to respond to what they know about their pupils and adapt their work to meet their needs. They also need to be able to guide or inform young people so that pupils are aware of what they have to do in order to make progress.

Levels in RE

Unlike the National Curriculum subjects, there are no statutory level descriptions for RE. The statutory document for RE which teachers in all schools should refer to, with the exception of voluntary aided schools, is the local agreed syllabus. Some agreed syllabuses have excellent information on assessment. Some provide thoughtful discussions of how assessment might be undertaken. Some provide an eight-level scale and some provide helpful, non-technical 'pupil speak' versions of their scales.

In an attempt to establish standards and improve the overall quality of agreed syllabuses, the DfES and the QCA in 2004 published *The Non-Statutory National Framework for Religious Education* (NFRE). This document builds upon an earlier advisory document (QCA 2000) by providing an eight-level scale. Early criticism of the NFRE scale claimed that there is a lack of clarity about what exactly levels 3, 4 and 5 mean, making it difficult to see any substantial difference between them. Also, levels 1 and 2, particularly with regard to AT2, are thought by some to lack challenge. In some respects levels 1 and 2 appear to be less demanding than the P levels 7 and 8 published by QCA in 2001.

P levels for RE were published in a booklet called *Religious Education: Planning, Teaching and Assessing the Curriculum for Pupils with Learning Difficulties* (QCA

2001). These levels are intended to outline early learning and attainment before level 1. Although the language in the P levels is quite clear, in contrast, many people have found the language used in the NFRE scales to be far from transparent. Without further commentary, the NFRE scales are probably not that clear to many specialist teachers of RE, let alone the many non-specialist teachers of RE that might be expected to use them. Bearing in mind these criticisms it is too early to say whether or not the non-statutory national framework scales will be widely used in local agreed syllabuses. The likelihood is that the NFRE scales will at least provide ideas which will be used as a basis for agreed syllabus assessment statements.

Progression in RE

In order for pupils to make progress in RE it is necessary for teachers of RE to be fairly clear about what 'making progress' in RE means. The most recent and promising attempts to describe progression in RE, as demonstrated in the NFRE, usually involve separating progress in *learning about religion* (AT1) from progress in *learning from religion* (AT2).

Learning about religion

When it comes to *learning about religion* it is possible to identify progression as involving three main steps. The first of these steps we can call 'recall'. The second step is 'description' and the third step is usually called 'understanding'.

Step 1: Recall

Recall takes place when pupils show some knowledge, usually factual knowledge, about religion. For example, a young person may look at a photograph and say, 'It's a mosque,' or they may recognise an artefact and say, 'It's a diva lamp.' Similarly, they may be able to recall the outline of a religious story. For example, a child may recall a simple version of the nativity story by reporting the following:

Jesus was born in a stable. There was no room at the inn.

Three wise men came.

This first step essentially shows disconnected knowledge. There is no evidence of an organised or connected body of knowledge but rather isolated pockets of knowledge often involving little more than single words. Rather like a dot puzzle – the dots are emerging on the page but the pupil hasn't really begun to connect up the dots.

Step 2: Description

A pupil who has achieved the second step onto the level of description shows knowledge which is now much more coherent and sustained. The pupil has begun to develop a pattern or web of knowledge. The dots are being joined up and are no longer simply disconnected facts. However, a pupil's knowledge is still largely limited to the factual. So, for example, if shown a picture of infant baptism, or if asked about the ceremony, a pupil may connect up three or four bits of knowledge. For example,

The man holds the baby. He pours water onto the baby's head.

There is a font which has water in it. It takes place in a church.

The pupil may not only have an emerging picture or web of knowledge about Christianity but there may be other developing pictures of other religious traditions. As more information about religions is learnt, pupils are able to attach this new information to their existing store of knowledge. So, if a pupil learns about fasting in Islam, this new information becomes linked to their existing store of knowledge about Islam resulting in an increasingly substantial and coherent picture of that faith.

Some children with learning difficulties have real problems integrating new information about a religion. This is often because they have virtually no existing mental framework onto which they can attach any new information about a faith. An important task for the teacher of RE is to find ways of helping such pupils to mentally organise and store new information so that pupils develop a coherent picture of each religion they study and are not left simply with a jumbled and confused array of half-remembered material.

Pupils with learning difficulties often have problems with description. This can be true in oral work but is particularly evident in written activities. For example, a pupil with learning difficulties in RE may:

- omit significant information

- use very simple sentences

- use long and rambling sentences, e.g. repetitive use of conjunctions – 'and then'

- present information in a non-logical order

- use certain words repetitiously, e.g. 'really nice', 'very big'

- fail to use appropriate religious vocabulary.

In order to support a child that has these sorts of difficulty the teacher of RE needs to establish whether the problem is due to limited learning about religion, in which case the child may need targeted support of a particular kind. For example:

- making information more vividly memorable

- providing additional scaffolding to help with the ordering of information

- providing recall activities to secure learning.

Or it may be that the child's difficulties are not primarily to do with learning about religion but have more to do with language and the organisation of ideas and information. If it is a general language difficulty, the child will be having the same sort of problems in other curriculum areas which demand similar language skills, for example, English, history and geography. If it is a more general difficulty with language, perhaps particularly written language, the nature of the support the child needs is different. For example:

- encouragement for the use of notes or diagrams to organise information prior to writing;

- the teacher modelling the process of composition;

- sharing composition, and encouraging the pupil to join in composing;

- support for writing using writing frames or a writing partner;

- encouragement for the use of drafting and re-drafting using word processing.

Of course, often pupils with learning difficulties struggle with a complex mix of problems involving both learning about religion and difficulty with ordering and communicating information and ideas.

Step 3: Understanding

The third step forward in learning about religion takes place when pupils begin to show understanding. When pupils have achieved this step, their knowledge about a religion is no longer confined to mere factual knowledge. Their knowledge is no longer limited to the overt external aspects of a religion, that is, what can be seen, heard or touched. Instead pupils now show awareness of the feelings, beliefs and emotions which are part of the experience of being religious. Pupils are no longer limited to knowledge which is about the 'what' and the 'where'. They are now able to offer answers which begin to explain religious life by responding effectively to 'why' questions.

For example, a person may be able to provide a sustained description of daily prayer in Islam. They may know that Muslims face in the direction of Makkah to pray, and that when they pray they stand, bow and prostrate. The pupil may know that as Muslims make these movements they recite particular words in Arabic. Yet, if asked why Muslims pray, a pupil may have no understanding of what prayer means to Muslims. They may not be aware of its status or significance within the faith. They may not be aware of the beliefs, emotions and feelings which Muslims associate with prayer. At the most extreme level of failure a person may think the ritual is of little more significance than a 'keep fit' exercise involving stretching and bending.

Children with learning difficulties often evade or underachieve tasks which call for understanding. For example:

- they avoid a loss of self-esteem and possible failure by using responses like, 'I don't know,' or by spending time on lower-order activities like description and apparently run out of time to undertake 'understanding' activities;

- they use circular responses which beg the question, e.g. 'They do it because it's their religion';

- they provide repetitive, non-specific responses, e.g. 'It's special to them,' or 'It's holy.'

Teachers need to be aware of these strategies and respond to them effectively. It is not unusual to see children continually use limited, brief answers, like 'They feel closer to God', to a whole array of questions about religious life. It is not unknown for teachers to reward such limited answers with misplaced praise, like 'Well done,' or 'Well tried.' Or else children are sometimes vaguely exhorted to strive for more insight, with comments like, 'Try to say more.' Alternatively it would be of more help to children if they were advised as to how they might improve their response to 'why' questions in RE. For example, children might be advised to

- avoid repetition of phrases, like 'it's special' or 'it's holy';

- make use of words which are more specifically used in different faith traditions, e.g. Islam – submission; Christianity – fellowship; Buddhism – compassion.

Learning from religion

The pattern of progress in *learning from religion* involves primarily a growing self-awareness rather than a growth of knowledge of the world out there. This growing self-awareness takes place in two senses.

Learning from religion – informing their own life

A child may *learn from religion* in the sense that they increasingly see how religion may inform their own life. A child may, for example, be able to recall, describe or explain the story of 'The Good Samaritan'. By doing so they would have demonstrated *learning about religion.* However, a child may also see ways in which the story may inform or have an application in their life. For example, a child may suggest that the story is telling them that to walk away from behaviour which is wrong, like bullying in the playground, is in itself wrong and that everyone has a responsibility to challenge bullying if it occurs.

Learning from religion – form their own judgements

But a child may *learn from religion* in a second sense, and that is, the study of religion may help a child to form their own judgements and arrive at a clearer and more informed understanding of their own beliefs and values.

Assessment in this area is sometimes incorrectly confused with the issue discussed earlier which is the inappropriateness of teachers making judgements about pupils' personal beliefs. This is not what is being suggested. *Learning from religion* doesn't involve telling children that their personal beliefs are right or wrong. Rather it is the process by which they arrive at their personal belief which the teacher of RE is concerned with. In other words, in RE the teacher encourages pupils to express their beliefs and values and to reflect on how they arrived at their judgement. In doing so pupils are helped to decide how they should make such judgements. For example, have they taken into account any available evidence? Are they being consistent? Have they considered the views of others? And are they aware of the consequences of their judgement?

When it comes to young people learning to articulate their own beliefs and values, we can again see a series of steps which shows progression. Step 1 occurs when a pupil is unaware of or uncertain about their own views. They may be asking significant questions like, 'How do we know God is real?' or 'Is there a secret to finding happiness?' but as yet they do not venture answers of their own. Step 2 can be seen as pupils express their views and are able to think of simple, supportive reasons. Step 3 occurs when pupils are able to provide a more sophisticated and informed, reasoned defence of their views.

Before young people even begin to make any of these steps there are earlier indications of progress in RE. For example, a pupil may demonstrate progress by listening attentively to the telling of a religious story or they may show some self-awareness by reflecting on what makes them happy or sad. These earlier steps are well described in the P levels in religious education (QCA 2001).

The way in which progression in AT1 and AT2 has been described provides a very general approach. Although many local agreed syllabuses adopt the form of progression described, not all of them do, and yet a school is obliged to conform to the local RE requirements. Increasingly the standards and expectations in agreed syllabuses take the form of either levels or end of key stage statements. Although there are some exceptions, the language of these statements tends to be rather academic, such that the sense is not always very easy to grasp. Even an experienced teacher of RE can be baffled by some agreed syllabus statements, let alone a child who has learning difficulties.

In order to begin to establish an effective assessment strategy which will help children with learning difficulties, it is necessary to involve pupils and actively give them some responsibility. Just as the classroom teacher needs to know what 'making progress' in RE means, so do the pupils. Sharing with pupils the local agreed syllabus levels or statements may help, but usually the language is so daunting that pupils cannot respond to them. Breaking down and simplifying the local standards into language the pupils can understand can help a great deal.

CHAPTER 7

Managing Support

A valuable resource

Over the last five years or so there has been a substantial increase in the number of adult support staff at work in classrooms. These are trained assistants (TAs), and the teacher of RE, just like the teacher of any other curriculum area, is wasting a valuable resource if they do not make effective use of any adult support made available to them. It is still the case that aside from a nod or a brief 'hello', a teaching assistant may be largely ignored by the mainstream classroom teacher. Sadly this can be just as true in the RE classroom as any curriculum area.

Wider contribution

Often a teaching assistant may have a central brief to support a particular child, or a group of children, that have special needs. However, in addition to that role many TAs understand their role in a much wider sense and are able and very willing to contribute to the quality of teaching and learning generally in the classroom. This can come about through the initiative of the teaching assistant. It is not unknown for a teaching assistant to enter into a contemporary RE classroom with little more than their childhood memory of RE, or memory of Sunday School classes, informing their expectations. Nevertheless, they quickly discover an unexpected world of religious diversity and thoughtful discussion. They may find the non-confessional aims of modern RE very appealing, such that they feel that they can and that they wish to contribute to the lessons more actively.

Although adult support staff may recognise the aims of the teacher of RE by observing what is happening in the classroom, it is usually better not to leave this unsaid, expecting the TA to surmise what is going on. Well before the lesson starts, it is of great help if the teacher of RE can spend some time providing a brief outline of what the lesson is about and what they are trying to achieve.

This enables the adult support staff to understand the lesson and puts them in a much better position to make a valuable contribution.

For example, in a lesson about murtis or images of gods used in Hinduism, the support staff might think that the main aim of the lesson is to develop accurate observation and recall. Believing this to be the case, the teaching assistant might ask the pupils they are working with to note how many arms or heads the image in front of them may have and to be satisfied if they answer correctly. The teacher, however, may be much more interested in encouraging the pupils to explore religious symbolism and is inviting pupils to consider what the image may be saying about the power of the divine symbolised by the image's many arms. Or the teacher may be interested in the belief that God has an all-seeing awareness of everything, symbolised by the many heads and eyes shown in the image. Of course, many observant teaching assistants can work out for themselves what the teacher is trying to achieve in the course of the lesson and improvise appropriate ways of supporting the teacher. But a proper professional discussion between the teacher and the teaching assistant prior to the lesson can help remove any misunderstanding.

Many teaching assistants will be able to draw upon their training and will find ways of supporting the teacher of RE during the course of the lesson. However, it is well worthwhile providing examples of how situations can be developed as they arise.

Encouraging reticent pupils

The teacher may show the class a number of images of mosques around the world and invite the pupils to comment on the dome as a common feature. Susan, a very shy girl who rarely speaks, may mutter, 'They look like onions.' The TA encourages Susan to speak up: 'Go on Susan, tell the class.' Susan repeats what she has said for the rest of the class to hear. This proves to be a very helpful contribution to the lesson. The teacher points out that the curves and shapes of natural objects like onions are often used in Islam. The children go on to learn that in Islam the curves of nature are believed to be curves designed by God.

Dropping helpful pointers

The class are invited to look at an image showing the earth from space. Working in pairs pupils are asked to think of a question the image raises for them. Shelley suggests that the planet looks 'lonely'. Her partner Dylan agrees, saying that the planet looks 'all on its own in the dark'. After a long pause the TA asks, 'If we are alone in the dark could we go and live anywhere else?' The pupils talk about pollution, the ozone layer and living on another planet. After a while the two pupils come up with the question, 'What must we do to save our planet from becoming too polluted for humans to live on?'

Starting the ball rolling

During a lesson on Jesus' concern for the outcast and the marginalised, based on the story of Jesus and Matthew the tax-collector, pupils in groups of three are asked to draw up a list of people who may feel outcast or rejected today. After a long pause the group seem unable to come up with any ideas. The TA mimes being elderly by pretending to have a shuffling gait and a bad back. The group start their list with 'old people' and then add 'young people with no jobs' and then add, 'refugees'.

Playing 'devil's advocate'

In groups of four the pupils are asked to discuss, 'What are the top things in life that bring happiness?' The group appear to largely agree, suggesting things like, 'friends', 'being loved' and 'having a family'. The TA joins in, saying, 'Get real . . . you need pots of money. Money can buy you happiness.' The discussion becomes more enlivened as the group counters the TA's contribution.

Echoing the teacher

In a series of lessons called 'Religion and the Rights of Women', pupils are asked to write a short statement giving their personal view on the question, 'Are Muslims right to ban beauty queen contests?' Sukvey writes a descriptive account of what traditional Muslim clothing for women looks like. The TA reminds Sukvey, 'Remember to give your personal view. Are Muslims right or wrong to ban beauty queen contests?'

Demonstrating for the teacher

The teacher explores with the pupils gestures used in Islam to symbolise respect for the Qur'an, such as washing hands before touching a Qur'an, wrapping the book in a cloth, placing it on a high shelf for safe keeping, placing it carefully onto a wooden stand off the floor for reading. As the teacher explains each of these gestures, the TA provides a demonstration.

In a more general sense TAs can help with the management of behaviour in an RE classroom. For example:

Sitting alongside a difficult child

Unnoticed by the teacher Shane may make several quiet verbal asides which distract or give offence to other children. For example, 'Look at him! He's got a tea towel around his head!' The TA changes position and sits closer to Shane. Shane recognises the signal and moderates his behaviour.

Troubleshooting

Georgina is becoming frustrated as the Passover bread (*matzot*) and mixture of apples, nuts, wine and cinnamon (*haroset*), placed on her table for the group to taste, has been eaten by other people in her group. The TA collects some more Passover bread and *haroset* from the teacher's desk and brings it to the table for Georgina to taste.

Supporting children that need specific help to access the lesson

Ricky has a particular difficulty with writing and often avoids getting started by using various avoidance activities, like distracting other pupils and leaving his seat to ask other pupils for a pen. The TA sits next to Ricky and encourages him to speak out loud his first sentence rather than write it down. The subject is Sikhism and arranged marriage. Ricky says, 'Well . . . arranged marriages seem strange but they work. Don't they!' With some further encouragement Ricky writes the first sentence: 'Arranged marriages may seem strange but many Sikhs find that they work.' With the help of a spellchecker the TA helps Ricky to spell 'arranged', 'strange' and 'Sikhs'.

Acting as a 'Thinking Partner'

During a lesson about Judaism and the Commandments the pupils are asked to think of a law that they would like to see passed. They are given two minutes' quiet thinking time. Adam draws a doodle. The TA asks Adam, 'What law would you like to see passed Adam?' Adam replies, 'Dunno.' 'Is there one thing in your street, in the playground, in the park, by the shops, anywhere, which could be made better?' 'Yeah,' says Adam, 'it should be a law to say you can go quad bike racing.' After further discussion Adam comes up with a law which grants funding to faith groups and non-governmental organisations to provide facilities and coaching in extreme sports for young people.

Management of resources

TAs can also help with the management of resources in the RE classroom. They can help a lesson move with pace and help avoid loss of concentration by distributing pencils or paper, holding up prompt cards, reading an extract from a book or perhaps operating equipment as in the following example:

> In a lesson which examines how God is discussed in contemporary music the pupils are to hear extracts from four separate songs. The first is Van Morrison singing 'Full Force Gale', which describes God as a strength in a crisis. This is to be followed by Madonna's 'Like a Prayer', which describes God as a mystery over which she has no control. The third song is Pink's use of the metaphor, 'God is a DJ' followed by George Harrison's sense of joy and love expressed in 'My Sweet Lord'. In between each song there is to be time for pupils to analyse and discuss. Each song extract is recorded on separate tapes. In order to try and bring about a seamless flow to the discussion the teacher asks the TA to operate the tape recorder, cue up each song and play the track when signalled.

Assessment and feedback

Teaching assistants can provide valuable information about what a particular child, or group of children, may learn during a lesson. We know that there is often a substantial gap between what teachers teach and what pupils learn.

A TA working closely with individual children may be able to identify how or why a child has failed to understand. Or they may observe that a child has distorted a particular idea, in a way of which the teacher may be quite unaware. For example, a teacher may have provided an excellent account of how Muhammad is believed by Muslims to be a prophet and that this is not the same as the Christian belief that Jesus is the Christ. A TA, while supporting children with special learning difficulties, may recognise that several of these children have not understood the distinction between 'The Prophet' and 'Christ' correctly. When questioned the children say things like, 'Muhammad is very special to Muslims, like Jesus is very special to Christians.'

Feedback from the TA about whether an idea has been understood, or lost in transmission, should be treated by the teacher as gold dust. If children are to effectively learn, the teacher of RE must know what has been understood, what has to be revisited, or how an idea may have to be tackled differently so as to avoid confusion. In order to encourage such feedback it is advisable for teachers to:

- provide briefing prior to a lesson

  Anticipating how an idea or a concept may be incorrectly grasped by children, brief the TA appropriately, prior to the lesson, so that they are alerted as to how children may fail to learn correctly;

- actively encourage feedback from the TA

  TAs can often be reluctant to give feedback to teachers even if they are very aware that children in the class have been completely unable to undertake a task or have failed to grasp vital information. They may fear that such observations will be regarded by the teacher as unwelcome criticisms. Teachers do need to make it clear that they value the TA's observations and that any post-analysis of a lesson will not be resented or treated in a cursory way.

Whole class teaching

Some adult support staff bring to the classroom skills and experiences which can be of enormous value to the teacher of RE. These skills and experiences can be drawn upon, if the adult support staff is willing, in a whole class setting.

First-hand knowledge of a religious tradition

A TA may well have almost unique, first-hand knowledge about a particular faith community. Such first-hand knowledge can be a tremendous asset in the RE classroom. With a little encouragement a TA may be persuaded to give a ten-minute presentation, either to a group of children, or perhaps for the whole class, on topics like:

- our family's celebration of Baisakhi
- my church group's annual visit to Lourdes
- my daughter's confirmation and first communion
- what it is like to fast during Ramadan
- how we pray at a Quaker meeting
- Puja and our family shrine to Krishna.

First-hand religious experience

Many people, and TAs are no exception, may have a fascinating story to tell about a spiritual or religious experience. Their story may have little to do with an explicit religious tradition. Nevertheless, if they are prepared to share the details of their experience in the classroom it can help bring alive for young people a real awareness of what often drives faith and commitment. Young people obviously have to be prepared for such stories and made aware that respecting the deeply held views and experiences of others is important. Having said that, young people are often very receptive to first-hand accounts of events:

- conversion experience

  perhaps following a period of some anxiety, an individual discovers reassurance and peace and senses the reality of God in their life;

- religious experience

  perhaps while having a country walk, an individual may have a mystical or a religious experience. For example, a person

  - hears an inner voice

  - senses a presence

  - has an out of body experience

  - receives a message from a deceased friend

  - senses a benevolent presence

  - has a deep feeling that nature is a unity

  - senses that in life everything will be okay;

- a spiritual journey

  an individual may have a story to tell of how their faith over the years has changed. Perhaps in childhood they accepted the teaching of their Catholic upbringing. Later in life they rebelled and found some satisfaction in a branch of Hinduism and eastern meditation. However, today they are generally sceptical and would describe themself as an atheist.

Social or community action

Some adult support staff may have experience in full- or part-time work for a charity or a community action project. Many such organisations are supported by people with a strong social conscience and have their roots in religious faith. A personal account of the day-to-day work, together with an attempt to explain something of the motives for getting involved, can provide the basis for a fascinating RE lesson.

For example, adult support staff can provide a valuable slot in an RE lesson based on their

- part-time work as a Samaritan

- Saturday morning work in a Sue Ryder shop

- VSO work in Uttar Pradesh

- sponsored cycle ride for Mencap

- previous employment in a hospice

- having a relative who has had to face the challenge of disability

- friends' experience of drug abuse.

Holidays and visits

Adult support staff, like many people today, are often reasonably well travelled. Clearly an RE lesson should be more than an indulgent look at an adult's holiday snaps. Nevertheless, with some thought and planning, and in the right setting, visits enjoyed by TAs both home and abroad can make a valuable contribution to an RE lesson. For example:

- celebrating Eid in Cairo

- visiting the Great Mosque in Tunis

- the day I went to Benares

- Mardi Gras in Rio de Janeiro

- the Passion Play in Oberammergau.

At the heart of these points is the principle of drawing TAs into the lesson in order to improve the learning process. Clearly this requires discussion and planning before the lesson begins. A rushed chat over coffee, three minutes before the lesson is due to start, is hardly likely to lead to the sharing of ideas and the professional discussion that is desired. When it comes to supporting children with learning difficulties, working with IEPs in mind can help. However, with the teacher and the TA working in partnership, identifying learning activities and specific targets for each lesson, a much better learning opportunity can be created and more genuine progress achieved.

CHAPTER 8

Real Pupils in Real Classrooms

We have so far looked generally at some of the issues which arise, and also at some of the strategies which might be used, in helping children that have special educational needs to make progress in RE. However, successful teaching is nearly always about understanding the needs of particular children and knowing what to do individually to develop their learning.

In this chapter we will look at case studies of individual children. Each individual case focuses on a particular type of educational need. It may be a child with a visual impairment, or it may be a child that has an emotional and a behaviour disorder, and offers some advice on how best to teach that child. Each case study has three sections: 'You will need to find out', 'You should consider' and 'Some strategies you or the TA could try'.

Effective teaching depends substantially upon the establishment of a relationship and a rapport between teacher and pupil. Being aware of a young person's educational need or of their particular impairment is important if you hope to teach them effectively. However, of even more importance is the individual child in themself; their likes and dislikes, their interests and hopes, their wishes and their fears. Every teacher will do well not to lose sight of the fact that through little conversations with children, by showing interest, by avoiding sarcasm or ridicule, by the giving of time, vital ingredients like trust and respect can be established. Without that trust and respect, trying to help another person learn will always be an uphill struggle.

Kuli Y7 – Hearing impairment

You will need to find out . . .

The degree of hearing loss Kuli has; for example, Kuli may have been diagnosed as having mild hearing loss. It may be however that Kuli's hearing impairment is much greater, in which case he may have been diagnosed as having moderate, severe or even profound hearing impairment.

You need also to find out if Kuli has his own personal FM radio-mike system. It may be that Kuli has such equipment but is uncomfortable using it and is reluctant to ask teachers to wear the mike. It may be that Kuli finds his FM system helpful but also has to rely substantially on his ability to decipher various visual clues like facial expressions and body language, and also on some lip-reading skill. Even with all that data it may be the case that Kuli misses crucial detail and is occasionally uncertain regarding instructions. It may also be the case that Kuli is reluctant to admit that he does not always follow what is going on but has a tendency to cover up, feign understanding and only rarely ask for help.

Kuli's greatest difficulty may however be in following the contributions made by others in the classroom who when speaking are not wearing the radio-mike. It may be that Kuli is experiencing RE which puts less emphasis on knowledge or ideas which come from the teacher. Instead, the expectation is that the pupils should contribute and show an increased willingness to clarify their own thoughts, ideas and views and share these with the other pupils. Kuli may therefore be finding that particularly during open discussion there can be a lively interchange and comments may come from unexpected members of the class. On such occasions Kuli may be finding it difficult to follow all of the contributions and so rarely feels able to join in himself.

IEP targets

You also need to find out if Kuli has an IEP, and if there is one, how the information or guidance provided can be used. Kuli may have clearly stated IEP targets. For example:

1. To work with a learning partner to ensure that instructions are understood.

2. To vary the learning partner in order to widen social opportunities.

3. To make at least one oral contribution in each lesson.

You should consider . . .

Regular consultation

In order to try and provide the best possible learning environment for Kuli you may wish to set up regular consultation meetings. This normally would involve the RE teacher setting aside some time every two or three weeks or so in order to consult with Kuli about his learning. Often this results in the student gaining confidence and gives them a sense that they have a voice in how they can make progress. It can also provide useful feedback for the teacher and may help them to reduce or even eliminate unconscious habits. For example:

- continuing to speak while turning to write on the board;

- standing in front of a window, creating a silhouette which hinders visual clues;

- leaving an OHP or perhaps an inkjet printer switched on when not in use, resulting in unnecessary background noise.

The room layout

Various classroom layouts and seating positions might be considered and a number of trials undertaken to see what works best. For example, it may be that by moving his seating position Kuli is able to avoid the movement of other members of the class, or is able to move closer to the teacher and so hear more clearly. Or it may be the case that with a little experimentation a horseshoe formation proves to be the most helpful layout enabling Kuli to observe most visual clues. Or it may be that during discussion the horseshoe formation can be quickly turned into a circle and that this greatly helps Kuli's ability to see who is speaking and to understand what is being said.

Some strategies you or the TA could try

Written information

Kuli may be provided with crucial written information either at the beginning or at certain appropriate moments in the course of the lesson. For example, Kuli may find it helpful to have

- an outline of the lesson, including the main aims;

- a list of any new words which will be introduced in the course of the lesson;

- any special class instructions, for example, a key question to be considered, e.g. 'In the story of Rama and Sita what lessons might be learnt from Rama?'

- a homework assignment.

A learning partner

Using the IEP target, a shortlist of learning partners for Kuli might be drawn up. A learning partner may help Kuli eliminate his occasional uncertainties about instructions. A learning partner may also help Kuli keep track of class discussions so that Kuli is better able to understand who is speaking and what is being said. As Kuli gains more confidence using a learning partner, a more random way of selecting members of the class to work with Kuli may be tried, in order to extend Kuli's social skills.

A word picture

Increasingly, sound may be used in an RE classroom in order to support learning. For example, students may have experienced

- a passage from the Qur'an being read

- the sound of a Gospel choir

- the chanting of a Chazan reading the Torah

- reflection supported by oriental sitar music.

When sound is being used in a major way to support learning, you may find that, rather than simply ignore Kuli on such occasions, it is possible to provide Kuli with a written word-picture of the sound. For example:

A female soloist sings out the words

> *Oh happy day, oh happy day*
>
> *When Jesus washed, when Jesus washed*
>
> *My sins away*
>
> *He taught me how, he taught me how*
>
> *To love and pray.*

A full choir joins in echoing each line the soloist sings.

There is a sense of gusto, power, life and great joy in the singing.

There is a powerful drumbeat and a lively melody giving the piece a

modern rock sound.

Such a strategy may of course be a limited substitute, but Kuli may well report that this is better than simply being ignored or pretending that there isn't a problem.

Harry Y7 – Specific learning difficulties

You will need to find out . . .

Harry may have a lot of ability in RE. However, this may not be at all evident to his RE teacher. Particularly in the first few weeks and months of pupils arriving in a secondary school, RE teachers often find themselves with very little in the way of useful information to make an adequate assessment of a pupil's ability in RE. Evidence like oral contributions, engagement in classroom activities, and information specific to RE from the primary feeder school, might all be in short supply.

Because of this, teachers of RE often make an initial assessment of a pupil's ability based on what data is available to them. In the first weeks of life in a secondary school this is often limited to a pupil's written work like homework or assignments undertaken during lessons. The evidence available to the teacher of RE may be writing assignments which are unfinished, low productivity, writing which is confused or poorly organised and words which are erratically or perhaps bizarrely spelt.

Viewing this evidence, teachers of RE have to identify those pupils who

- are poorly motivated

  These are pupils who underachieve in RE but in other curriculum areas respond much more positively and produce work of a much higher standard.

- have a general learning difficulty

  These are pupils who have a general cognitive difficulty and so find it hard to recall or organise information, or understand ideas, or grasp concepts. Because of this general difficulty they are almost certainly also having difficulty with other subjects which require cognitive skills.

- have a specific learning difficulty

  This is the situation with Harry. Harry in his RE lessons is not being 'sloppy' or 'unco-operative'. Nor is he necessarily of limited ability in RE. He could be highly gifted. The problem is that Harry is being asked to undertake assignments in RE primarily through the medium of the written word, and Harry's problem is specifically with the written word, not with RE.

Diagnostic analysis

Harry's specific learning difficulty with words needs to be diagnostically analysed. This means that the school needs to find out what strategies Harry uses when he is asked to write – for example, how he plans, how he sets about composition, how he attempts to spell, what sort of errors he makes and what might be the source of those errors. The school should also look at how Harry revises his work, whether in fact he ever redrafts his work, and if so what he does during the redrafting stage.

You should consider . . .

Scaffolding writing

It may be that Harry's greatest difficulty when faced with a writing assignment is that he has a problem getting started. In order to help him develop his skill and build his confidence, it may be necessary to provide writing tasks which are very clear and structured. This may take the form of providing scaffolding or a skeleton. For example:

When I entered the Sikh gurdwara I thought . . . .

Inside I saw . . . .

The thing that struck me most . . . .

One thing our Sikh guide said . . . .

Later on we visited the langar, where . . . .

Sikhs believe . . . .

What I gained most from the visit was . . . .

Fluency and repetition

It may be that Harry has a tendency to write in short sentences so that his work lacks fluency. For example:

They pray everyday.

They face Mecca.

They pray to Allah.

It is a commandment.

It is in the Qur'an.

Harry may need particular help so that he learns how sentences can be combined. He may need help in order for him to recognise how his writing is repetitious and how this can be overcome. For example:

Muslims pray to Allah everyday. When they pray they always face Mecca.

The commandment to pray is found in the Qur'an.

Writing as a process

It may be the case that Harry needs to be encouraged to think that when undertaking a writing task he is not expected to produce an accurate and neat product at the first attempt. Writing should be seen as a process beginning with talking over ideas and sketching out some initial thoughts. Work can be edited and revised several times. In support of this idea of writing as a process Harry's RE teacher may wish to encourage him not to use an exercise book but to use a loose-leaf folder. This will make it possible for Harry not to be always reminded of past failures but to store final drafts in which he can take pride. (See notes on CD about the writing process)

If a word processor can be accessed, this can be of enormous help to Harry. It will enable him to edit, erase and refine his work through several drafts, achieving a final quality product.

Some strategies you or the TA could try . . .

Specific strategies for overcoming difficulties with spelling

Harry may have a real difficulty with spelling. He may spell some words quite erratically but nevertheless show some awareness of a correspondence between letter patterns and sound. For example, 'becos' (because), 'bibel' (Bible), 'juwes' (Jews). However, some words may be spelt in a much more bizarre way as he mistakes the letter name for the sound, for example, 'gsos' (Jesus) or 'yl' (while). These sorts of difficulties are unlikely to correct themselves unless the issue is faced and Harry is explicitly taught spelling skills. Indeed, unless tackled the problem is likely to get worse as Harry may increasingly find his spelling embarrassing and simply withdraw as a 'reluctant writer' or become angry and frustrated and develop a behaviour problem.

Strategies that may help Harry improve his spelling:

- Draw up a list of words Harry frequently misspells. Some of these may be general words 'sed' (said), but some may be more specific to RE, e.g. 'religous' (religious), 'Buddism' (Buddhism), 'gud' (good), 'beleve' (believe).

- Establish a systematic programme of learning a list of words Harry frequently misspells.

- Encourage Harry to make an active effort to remember every detail of a targeted word. Harry should look carefully at how the word should be spelt, but also he should look carefully at how he tends to misspell the word.

- While speaking the word, quietly practise writing the word from memory. Attempt to learn each word by eye, ear and hand, not just by eye alone. See the word, say the word, feel the word, write the word. (See look, say, cover, write, check prompt on accompanying CD)

- Make use of a progress chart in order to plot the number of new words learnt each week.

- Make use of an electronic spellchecker so as to avoid frustration when writing.

Megan Y10 – Wheelchair user

You will need to find out . . .

Consultation

Consultation should be a major feature of a school's educational provision for Megan, and this applies just as much in the RE classroom as elsewhere. The fact that Megan has a mobility impairment does not mean that she has a similar impairment when it comes to speaking, learning, thinking or feeling. It is important not to patronise, condescend or make assumptions about Megan's preferences without exploring her views on the matter.

Physical access

If Megan's RE lessons are taking place in a classroom she hasn't used before, it will be necessary to find out if this is presenting her with unforeseen access problems. Obvious modifications like ramps, lifts and toilet facilities may be in place generally within the school. However, Megan may be encountering particular access problems which she should be consulted about in order that improvements or solutions can be found.

Megan should also be consulted about where she wishes to place herself in the classroom. She may, for example, find it helpful if an easily accessible space in the classroom is reserved.

Preferred learning style

It will also be necessary to find out Megan's particular strengths and weaknesses as a learner. It is important when looking at Megan not only to see the wheelchair but also to see Megan as a young person with her own particular strengths and weaknesses and preferences as a learner. She may principally use mind-mapping, pictures and diagrams to grasp and communicate ideas. It may be that she has a strong social conscience and a particular interest in moral issues, or in evangelical Christianity, or in questions about existence and destiny. In which case this information may be just as important, perhaps more important to bear in mind when teaching Megan, than anything to do with her as a wheelchair user.

You should consider . . .

When teaching Megan there are a number of do's and don'ts which you should consider. These may not be very specific to religious education but they are nevertheless important. For example:

- When talking to Megan, sit beside her so that your eyes are at the same level.

- Sit free of Megan's wheelchair and avoid leaning on it. Megan may well regard her wheelchair as part of her personal space.

- Don't assume that Megan needs assistance, for example in accessing resources or equipment. She may well enjoy exercising her independence and not want others always doing things for her.

- At the same time be alert in case Megan does need assistance – for example, with accessing books or resources which are on a high shelf, carrying objects or holding a door open.

- Give consideration to how Megan can best be helped to participate in classroom strategies which anticipate movement around the classroom. For example, forming a discussion circle, undertaking a role-play, forming a group to work with.

- Also give consideration to how Megan can participate in visits and out-of-school activities, such as visiting a local synagogue, or undertaking a survey on local attitudes to religion .

- If Megan is being prepared for some form of national accreditation in RE, find out if the examining authority permits additional time or rest breaks. This is likely to depend on Megan's specific disability. Advice can usually be gained from the examination board's examination officer and it is possible that medical evidence may be required.

Some strategies you or the TA could try

As pupils enter into Key Stage 4 it is increasingly likely that they will be undertaking an RE course which is intended to prepare them for some form of national accreditation. Although success in a religious studies GCSE or Certificate of Achievement might seem like incentive enough from the point of view of the teacher, this is not necessarily the view adopted by students. The exam carrot is not enough. Instead, the most successful Key Stage 4 RE teaching programmes attempt to achieve the following.

Minimise writing

Writing which is little more than note-taking, on the grounds that this is needed for revision purposes, is often resented by young people, including young people who are wheelchair uses. If essential information has to be made available it is better to provide printed copies of such information which students may read and store for future reference.

Encourage discussion

RE provides many opportunities for young people to engage in discussion in order that they can learn how to form and articulate their views. Teachers of RE should maximise opportunities for such discussion. Megan may need some encouragement in some discussions, but all participants should be made aware of certain rules, like

- listening to others

- taking turns

- using the language of courtesy.

  Class discussions nearly always go better if

- the subject under discussion is topical and relevant;

- the students have had some say about the question or motion to be discussed;

- the contributions from very vocal individuals are restricted, encouraging less confident students to make a contribution;

- the teacher makes it clear that they are 'active listeners' to the discussion and are not 'active participants' wishing to push the discussion towards a particular conclusion.

Vary the format

Attempt to plan lessons which take the students by surprise by avoiding the same format or routines. Role play may seem like a novel way to learn, but if role play becomes a repeated strategy it quickly becomes predictable and loses its impact. Attempt to surprise your students, with

- *visiting speakers* – a local hospital chaplain explains their day-to-day work;

- *problem-solving* – Should Mr and Mrs Williams have their baby baptised?

- *mock trials* – the British media on trial, 'Is it guilty of demonising Islam?'

- *an imaginary TV interview* – 'If Jesus were alive today' – the David Dimbleby Interview;

- *expert in role* – an atheist scientist on the origin of life;

- *design an advert* – plan a 25-second TV advert for Buddhism.

In all these activities Megan should be encouraged to play a full and active part. She should be given opportunities to take a lead – and not be seen merely as someone who is helped out by making sure she has a good view of what others in the classroom are doing.

Steven Y8 – Emotional and behavioural disorder (EBD)

You will need to find out . . .

Steven may show his emotional and behavioural disorder in a variety of ways. The teacher of RE may find that Steven has a range of social, aggressive and disruptive difficulties. For example, he may

- be very impulsive

- easily become distracted, restless and inattentive

- have poor social relationships

- often be off-task, use verbal abuse or verbally bait other students or the teacher

- be threatening, physically aggressive, easily angered, violent.

All too often pupils who exhibit such behaviour experience traumatic lives outside of school in which tension and aggression are the norm. In such an environment a young person may become destructive and rebellious. They may have difficulty in establishing close relationships and suffer from low self-esteem. Knowledge of Steven's home circumstances can be a revelation to some of his teachers and may help them to arrive at a much more balanced assessment of his behaviour.

However, even if Steven does have a very difficult home background, that does not mean that the situation is hopeless and nothing can be done. Research into effective schools indicates that schools can play a major role in either helping or hindering young people with EBD.

RE teachers that are most effective in teaching young people like Steven usually find that their task is made easier when they teach in schools which have

- an effective senior management which provides direction for all staff. They take an interest in RE and support the subject, particularly in terms of time-tabling, accommodation and staffing, and are committed to the development of good quality teaching and learning;

- a whole school policy on behaviour;

- a 'critical mass' of staff that support and practise the school's behaviour policy.

You will need to know if there is a policy in the school if Steven, or pupils like Steven, harass or bully other children. For example, is there a 'cool-off zone' or a 'time-out plan' and if there is, how does it operate? Does Steven have an 'individual behaviour plan' or a 'contract', and if not does the school have a system in place for generating one? Has the school in place a system for teaching Steven anger-management skills? Has Steven been advised about what he should do if he finds himself getting angry or how he might avoid such a situation arising? Are there prescribed classroom rules covering situations in which Steven typically may be experiencing difficulty? For example, are there clear rules like, 'lining up', 'coming in' or 'going out' rules? Does the school have 'talking', 'hands up', 'swearing', 'eating', 'arriving late' or 'coats off' rules? Are these rules being applied consistently throughout the school? Does Steven need additional support or training in order that he understands these rules and what is expected of him?

Or is the expectation perhaps that each teacher will negotiate such rules for themselves with each of their classes, in order to encourage ownership of the rules? As RE often involves discussion of controversial or sensitive issues, it can be useful for every teacher of RE to negotiate with their classes a suitable 'positive language rule', or a 'non-put-down rule' or a 'racist language rule'.

You should consider . . .

A behaviour profile

It may be that a real step forward in helping Steven to manage his behaviour can be achieved if a 'behaviour profile' of Steven is undertaken. A 'behaviour profile' is a formal study of Steven's behaviour. For example, is Steven disruptive in virtually all of his lessons, or is it just RE and one or two other lessons? Does Steven have particular bad-days? For example, is there a pattern of misbehaviour on Mondays or Fridays, or on afternoons, or following particular lessons?

Curriculum design

Even if Steven's disruptive behaviour is not confined to just RE, it is still necessary to make sure that the RE curriculum design is appropriate. Some RE schemes of work continue to contain areas of study which are of doubtful relevance to many young people today. It may be that Steven is particularly rebellious if he is expected to learn about the geography of ancient Israel, or become familiar with ancient Polynesian creation stories, or explain what difference there may be between an Ansate, a Maltese, a Celtic, a Papal and a Lorraine cross.

Far from reinforcing knowledge, some RE tasks, like 'Draw a picture of Jesus' entry into Jerusalem', 'Copy out the words of the Muslim call to prayer', or 'Decorate your Succoth Card with Jewish symbols', are little more than ways of keeping young people occupied while the clock ticks down. Frustration at his inability to draw Jesus on a donkey and his feeling that, even if he could, what purpose would it serve, could be a contributory factor in Steven's distracted behaviour and frequent task refusal.

Some strategies you or the TA could try

Steven's behaviour may be aggravated by poor classroom management. RE teachers are not saints, and just like any other human being, an RE teacher may find themselves aggravated by Steven's behaviour. Arising from a trivial incident

Steven may swear and react aggressively, 'Give me back my pen you s _ _.' He may engage in argument, back-chat of defiance, 'I'm not talking! You're always picking on me. I'm not working with her!' The temptation is to think that you must use counter power to show that you are in charge. The teacher may feel that what is needed in such a situation is an angry and loud retort, 'How dare you talk like that in my classroom!' Many teachers think that by a demonstration of their power Steven will get the message and this will correct his behaviour.

By showing reactive anger are you helping to defuse the situation? Or are you, by entering into a power struggle with Steven, backing him in public into a corner, which simply increases the tension and only makes the situation worse? There are alternative strategies and ways of managing anger and avoiding possible conflict. For example, avoid shouting, yelling or threatening Steven. This usually will only result in more hostility and anger from Steven and is very likely to damage the relationship you are trying to establish to ensure learning. Young people very quickly see a contradiction between a teacher who shouts in the classroom and yet, a few moments later, expects them to consider issues to do with spiritual, social and moral development. Instead:

- Train yourself to talk calmly, and be assertive but not aggressive.

- Avoid a public rebuke; talk to Steven in close proximity, or if possible away from his peers.

- Focus on the primary behaviour, not on secondary behaviour.

- Remind Steven of the school or classroom rule, making it clear that compliance is a requirement, not a request, 'Remember the rule Steven, no shouting. Thanks.'

- If possible require Steven to take responsibility for his behaviour by giving him a clear choice, 'Either sit down Steven and continue with your work or go to the "cool-off" room. It's your choice Steven.'

- Withdraw and avoid any further confrontation or rewarding Steven's aggressive behaviour with his wish to have attention.

- If possible catch Steven being good and avoid sarcasm or irony. 'Thanks for putting your hand up Steven. How can I help?'

- Follow up afterwards after an opportunity to cool-off.

Steven may frequently drift off-task or task-refuse during his RE lessons. He may challenge the work or bait the RE teacher. For example, he may shout out, 'RE is rubbish!' or 'I hate RE.' It is easy for an RE teacher to take this personally and feel that they have to enter into a justification of the subject. In most cases this is not appropriate. If a student has serious uncertainties about what RE is about, this cannot be resolved with a two-minute discussion in the middle of a lesson. Steven may be involved in attention-seeking, and by indulging his desire, while you attempt to explain the virtues of RE, the likelihood is that he will employ similar behaviour the next time he wants a dose of attention. If Steven has a genuine concern about the role of RE in his education the issue can be pursued with Steven after the lesson. Or perhaps the issue can be taken up on another occasion in a class discussion during which Steven would have an opportunity to more fully present his reservations. Instead try to find a strategy for dealing with a challenge of this sort. For example:

- Remain calm, avoid taking the comment personally as a challenge to your role in the school. The likelihood is that Steven tells other subject teachers, 'Maths is boring!' or 'I really hate history.'

- Show that you are a human being and you acknowledge his feelings, 'Doing work you hate can be irritating, Steven.'

- Direct Steven back to the immediate task, 'Can you do the work, Steven? If not, I could give you some help, or I could find a partner for you to work with.'

Jenny Y7 – Down's Syndrome (DS)

You will need to find out . . .

Initially Jenny's RE teacher will need to find out in what ways, and to what extent, she has general cognitive and learning difficulties, which are typically associated with Down's Syndrome. The degree of learning difficulty a person with DS may experience can vary enormously. It can range from mild to severe. This learning difficulty will lead to a development gap between Jenny and most of her peers. However, although this gap is likely to widen as she gets older, the evidence suggests that Jenny will nevertheless do better academically and socially working in an inclusive mainstream setting.

Jenny's cognitive and learning difficulties in RE may be due to a number of factors, all or only some of which Jenny may have. For example, Jenny may have a

- short-term auditory memory
- speech and language impairment
- hearing impairment
- visual impairment
- fine and gross motor skill impairment
- thinking, reasoning and generalisation difficulties.

Within the school the most likely sources of information about Jenny's specific learning difficulties will be Jenny herself. Jenny might well be very happy, indeed keen, to talk about what she can do and what she finds difficult. Listening to Jenny and giving her an opportunity to have a voice is important also for the development of self-esteem and social skills.

As well as Jenny herself, other sources of valuable information and advice will include

- Jenny's parents
- the school's SENCO
- Jenny's IEP
- any teaching assistants that have experience of working with Jenny
- primary school transition information.

You should consider . . .

Regular meetings

In order to plan activities and support for Jenny during her RE lessons you should consider establishing regular meetings with the teaching assistant. The teaching assistant is likely to know Jenny well, but they are unlikely to have much specialist knowledge of RE. Regular meetings with the TA are not undertaken as acts of mere professional courtesy. They are likely to greatly increase both the teacher's and the teaching assistant's effectiveness during lessons. However, it is important that the TA is not seen as belonging to Jenny, but is understood as belonging to the whole class. It is also important that Jenny's RE experience is not with the TA alone but that in each lesson Jenny receives some personal interaction with the RE teacher as well.

Planning meetings with the RE teacher and the TA might be part of a wider schedule of meetings which also involve the SENCO, other curriculum class teachers and support staff. These meetings provide an opportunity to plan, feedback and monitor Jenny's progress generally.

Verbal instructions

You should also consider ensuring that Jenny understands what you say in the classroom. If Jenny has a short-term auditory memory it is advisable to avoid long verbal instructions. Even relatively short verbal instructions or spoken information, if possible, should be divided up into more manageable chunks enabling Jenny to have time to assimilate what has been said.

In addition to the dividing up of spoken information, it may be helpful if Jenny can have such instructions or information repeated to her, or perhaps reinforced by the use of written or visual guidance.

Visual cues

The written word can help Jenny as it provides visual support, which reinforces the spoken word. For this reason Jenny is likely to find it helpful if you provide visual support in the form of flash cards, key words or picture cues. So for example the class may be asked to recall three things they remember about the Buddha from the previous lesson. Jenny is given three picture cues: the first shows the story of the boy Buddha and the wounded swan, a second shows the Buddha's enlightenment, and a third shows the story of the Buddha and the charging elephant.

Differentiation

Differentiated activities and resources, if they can be appropriately prepared, should also be considered. Handouts and worksheets continue to be a popular resource used by teachers of RE. Many teachers of RE find that available textbooks provide information which does not quite fit their learning intentions and so continue to prepare material of their own. However, handouts if not prepared properly can be a source of confusion and frustration. If thoughtfully differentiated they can be a valuable way of helping Jenny to make progress.

Any handouts or worksheets distributed to the class may in Jenny's case be in a larger font format. Although Jenny may be a good visual learner she may have difficulty reading standard font sizes, like 11 or 12 points, due to visual impairment. The text may be simplified so as to contain the essential information. Particular attention should be given to ensuring a simple, clear layout and, if suitable, picture cues.

Jenny's homework should also be differentiated, particularly if she is set an assignment which requires writing. Not only might Jenny find that because of her cognitive difficulties, understanding the homework could be a problem, but also poor muscle tone and loose joints (hypotonia) mean that her ability and the speed at which she writes are likely also to be affected.

A home-school book, in which Jenny's homework is written down for her, may prove to be helpful. It can also provide a valuable way in which Jenny's parents can provide helpful feedback and be more effectively involved in helping Jenny to make progress.

Seating arrangements

If Jenny does have both a visual and a hearing impairment you may wish to encourage her to sit nearer the front of the class.

Some strategies you or the TA could try

The development gap between Jenny and most of her peers means that the activities and tasks set for her will be less challenging, but at the same time she should not find herself patronised by tasks which are trivial. What this might mean is that some pupils undertake tasks which require analysis. For example:

'Why do many Hindus worship using an image of a god?'

Or perhaps the task requires evaluation, which is set in a challenging abstract context. For example:

'Does an image aid or hinder worship?'

Meanwhile, Jenny may still be following the same curriculum content although her task requires mainly description rather analysis. For example:

'In the photo Ravi is worshipping the goddess Lakshmi.

Describe what you can see.'

Jenny's work has to be carefully monitored, as it is all too easy to provide an over-diluted curriculum. It is quite possible that Jenny can express her own view, or evaluate, as long as the question is asked in a context which is concrete and avoids too much abstraction, or if the question is put in an imaginative way.

For example:

'Why is Ravi worshipping Lakshmi?' [or] 'If Ravi didn't worship Lakshmi

what would he miss?'

Jenny may be further aided in her response to such tasks by giving her more time to make a written response. Alternatively, she may be permitted to give a verbal response. It is important that you give her thinking time so she can consider her answer and sufficient time to say all that she wants to say. Jenny may also have speech difficulties. Because of this, her RE teacher should avoid anticipating her answer by finishing off her sentences for her.

Getting the level of challenge right for Jenny is particularly important. Differentiation in RE does not mean that while others are asked to think about the motives and purposes behind Hindu worship, Jenny is spending time copying and colouring-in a picture of a Hindu god. Cloze activities may be a strategy that can be used, but if they involve merely slotting in one-word answers to complete a sentence, they are of dubious educational value. An RE curriculum should never become so diluted that Jenny is never asked to evaluate or offer her own opinion. Jenny may be helped to express her views using strategies like

- continuum line

- multi-choice

- writing frame.

Continuum line

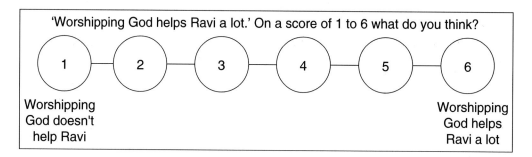

Multi-choice

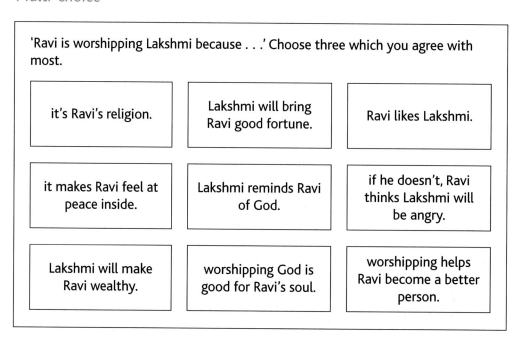

Writing frame

My views about worship

I think worship helps Ravi because ....

Worship is like ....

An example of how worship can help Ravi is ....

Some people think worship doesn't help people because ....

But I don't agree with this view because ....

My views about worship

I think worship does not help people because ....

Some people believe that worship can help a person by ....

An example of how some people think worship can help a person is ....

But I don't agree with this because ....

Instead of worship I think ....

Such strategies should not be seen as achieving final outcomes but as springboards to further discussion and further refinement of thought. Jenny's ability to understand or form an opinion may be a good deal better than her ability to express her understanding or structure an argument. As a result, Jenny's cognitive and reasoning skills may easily be underestimated and so her progress held back.

As Jenny progresses into Key Stage 4, it is also important not to exclude her from the possibility of some form of national accreditation. If GCSE is judged to be inappropriate, other forms of accreditation should be explored including Certificate of Achievement in Religious Studies and Entry Level qualifications.

Bhavini Y9 – Visual impairment

You will need to find out . . .

There are many different degrees of visual impairment ranging from low vision to blindness. Bhavini's RE teacher will need to find out the extent of Bhavini's visual impairment. A low-vision student, perhaps with the use of magnification equipment, may be able effectively to read print. Even if Bhavini is blind the extent to which her impairment impedes her learning may vary depending on her background and training. For example, she may have a high degree of proficiency in Braille. Or she may have a well developed auditory memory, which enables her to recall conversations or spoken information, with a high level of accuracy.

If Bhavini does have some functional sight and is able to see print you will need to find out what size print Bhavini is best able to see. It may be that a large print setting of 16–18 points suits Bhavini, or that she finds a particular font like Arial visually much more comfortable than any other. If in the classroom you have available an interactive whiteboard, it may be that following some research Bhavini finds that her visual discrimination is improved through the use of colour. For example, she may find it easier to see text in a particular colour, perhaps dark blue on yellow, rather than the standard default setting.

You will also need to find out if Bhavini finds it helpful to use relatively inexpensive equipment like a magnification lens, additional lighting or a sloping reading platform. It may be that Bhavini prefers to sit away from glaring light, for example by avoiding seats near a window. She may alternatively find it helpful to sit closer to the front of the classroom. It may also be the case that within the school Bhavini is familiar with certain working arrangements which she both prefers and finds helpful. For example, she may be used to working with a particular sighted partner or partners, or perhaps more generally finds paired or group work greatly helps her learning. There may be established practices in the school which you would want to maintain. For example, Bhavini may usually leave the classroom a little early in order to give her extra time to get to her next lesson.

The source of much of this information will be available from the SENCO. However, it is also well worthwhile spending some time with Bhavini talking about her learning and how her learning can best be supported. This need not be a single, one-off meeting. Setting aside some time on a regular basis in order to speak to Bhavini can be of great help. Such regular meetings can

- provide useful information which can help inform how Bhavini can best be taught;

- provide useful feedback about what Bhavini has learnt and where additional support may be needed;

- engage Bhavini more fully in her own learning and so help her to take more responsibility for her learning.

You should consider . . .

Alternatives to using text

There are ways of conveying ideas and information in the RE classroom other than using text. Many RE lessons continue to make extensive use of reading and writing activities. The mistaken belief is that by reading information from a book or a handout is an effective way of achieving learning. The value of the written word in the development of many of the world's religions has been immense, but the effectiveness of the written word in the RE classroom is greatly exaggerated.

That doesn't mean that the teacher of RE shouldn't continue to help Bhavini access the printed or the written word, for example by providing

- Bhavini with a reader or by offering to read the text for her;

- tapes of text which Bhavini can listen to, using earphones.

However, it does mean that the teachers should be wary of excessive use of strategies which rely heavily on reading and writing in the RE classroom. Although many RE textbooks contain descriptions of religious rituals, festivals, beliefs and stories, reading such material often has very little appeal for young people, and so it is not surprising that the quality of recall or of understanding is often disappointing. Much more memorable strategies involve young people, not in reading or writing, but instead having them get to their feet and physically participating or speaking. For example:

- a narrated reconstruction of what happens in a gurdwara during an Amrit service;

- playing games like dreidel and eating food like cheese blintzes and potato latkes associated with the celebration of the festival of Hanukkah.

- preparing and performing a mock outside TV broadcast on a topical issue of religious significance, e.g. performances of a play which gave religious offence are cancelled following a violent protest.

Bhavini will often be able to engage in such classroom activities unhindered by any difficulty she may have in seeing print or in writing text. By doing so it is also more likely that all of the students will have a much stronger memory of the events or ideas being studied than would be achieved by the use of reading and writing strategies alone.

Generally increasing the opportunities for paired and group work may be of help to Bhavini, particularly if she finds it helpful to have a sighted partner to help her with aspects of her work.

ICT support

You should also consider how ICT may be used to support Bhavini's learning, for example, voice recognition software would permit Bhavini to record her ideas and have the PC convert her spoken words into a written text. Screen reader software would make it possible for any text Bhavini might be researching to be accessed, as the text would be converted into a sound recording on a PC.

Some strategies you or the TA could try

The advantages of using kinaesthetic activities, which involve simulating, in ways which are appropriate, rituals, ceremonies and festivals, have already been advised. However, difficult religious concepts and beliefs can also be made clearer to young people through the use of physical participation, which equally for Bhavini as for other students could be an effective learning strategy.

Pass the Message

This activity is designed to help young people understand the Islamic concept of revelation and the role of the prophets in Islamic thought. Pass the Message involves dividing the class into two halves. One half invent a message. This message is passed to the other half of the class via an appointed messenger who repeats the message verbatim. Individuals in the receiving half of the class are asked to role-play ways in which a person may respond to the message over a period of time. For example, some mock the message, others ignore it, some write the message down verbatim, learn the message by heart and act on the message, while others attempt to memorise the message but distort the message over a period of time. Meanwhile the other half of the class are given a similar task but their messenger loosely extemporises the message.

The Gauntlet and Candle

The Gauntlet and Candle activity is similarly intended to help young people to better understand the Jewish belief that the original Abrahamic–Mosaic concept of a single, just God has faced many historical threats to its survival. The survival of this concept of God, indeed its widespread adoption, is thought to be a sign of its truth and of God acting in history. Most of these threats came from the powerful and clearly successful neighbouring empires like the Egyptians, the Assyrians, the Philistines, the Babylonians, the Greeks and the Romans. The class is divided into six groups, each group representing a neighbouring empire. Each group is then positioned in order to form a gauntlet or corridor. A volunteer carries a lighted non-extinguishable candle slowly through the gauntlet. Members of the gauntlet, as the candle passes, unsuccessfully attempt to blow out the candle. At the end of the gauntlet the candle is used to light two other candles to represent how the Abrahamic–Mosaic concept of God has become central to other traditions like Islam and Christianity.

Tactile learning

Bhavini's learning can be supported by generally increasing tactile learning opportunities. So instead of merely being told about the Christian tradition of eating pancakes on Shrove Tuesday and making palm leaves in preparation for Palm Sunday, pupils are much more fully engaged, and are more likely to learn, if they actually eat a pancake and handle a palm cross.

Similarly, when it comes to using religious artefacts like a Buddhist prayer wheel, a Hindu puja bell, Christian incense, a Sikh kangha, or a Sabbath spice box, such items should not be kept locked away in a display cabinet. Nor should they only be held aloft for only sighted students to catch a glimpse of. Instead, following some discussion of how non-members of a religious tradition might show appropriate respect for the beliefs of others, such items should be passed around for pupils to hold and feel so that they acquire a multi-sensory memory of different faith traditions.

Additional strategies that can be undertaken include:

- if slides or images are being used, provide a description of those images;

- make verbal instructions clear and avoid vague directional statements like 'over there', 'here' or 'this';

- if you ask Bhavini a question begin by using her name, e.g. 'Bhavini, what did your group find out about Islamic beliefs about stewardship?'

- ensure that resources and materials like pencils, rulers and paper are stored in the same place so that Bhavini can exercise, where she can, independence in the classroom.

Susan Y10 – Autistic Spectrum Disorder

You will need to find out . . .

You will need to find out the main characteristics and severity of Susan's disorder. It is possible that Susan has been diagnosed with Asperger's Syndrome. This might show itself in a complete lack of eye contact and an unwillingness to mix with other students during break and lunchtime. Nevertheless, Susan may have a highly focused intellect and may be able to master a complex line of argument.

However, Susan's ASD might give rise to very different characteristics. The school's SENCO may be very familiar with Susan's disorder and may have a very helpful IEP. Susan's RE teacher needs to be aware of her IEP and use it as a basis for both the planning and the delivery of her RE lessons.

Susan may have a problem with motor-control, resulting in poor handwriting. Because of this it may help Susan to be encouraged whenever possible to word-process her work.

You will also need to know if Susan has any history of unexpected or difficult behaviour. She may under some circumstances appear non-cooperative. She may appear to be deliberately disruptive, given on occasions to muttering or other verbal habits. Awareness of such characteristics can help prevent a teacher misconstruing Susan's behaviour and responding inappropriately.

You should consider . . .

A quiet area

Susan may feel more comfortable and be able to work better if a quiet, undisturbed area within the RE classroom can be arranged. Or the lighting may need to be adjusted in some way, or perhaps Susan is fixed on something which may seem inconsequential like a squeaking window catch or a creaking chair which can relatively easily be resolved.

Specialist interest

You should also consider if Susan has a particular area of specialist interest. For example, Susan may have a particular interest in animals, in the environment, in astronomy and space, or in the structure of buildings. It may be that her special interest can seem like a preoccupation. Nevertheless, it could be used as the basis for a special RE project which Susan may wish to pursue avidly. This need not be a solitary pursuit. With encouragement Susan may wish to work with a partner, or may wish to share her findings with others, or indeed with the rest of the class.

Need for routine

Susan may also have a need for routine, and any alterations in this routine may be unsettling. This does not mean that Susan cannot be involved in RE visits or that visiting speakers must be avoided. It may be helpful if other adults that are likely to meet Susan for the first time on such occasions should be appropriately briefed. Susan's behaviour may seem odd, and an adult, on first acquaintance, might misconstrue the situation.

It may be that any changes in the routine need to be explained to Susan as fully as possible. Simply saying, 'Next week we've got a visitor' may cause Susan to react with alarm. This may be avoided by providing much more information; for example, 'Next Wednesday Mrs Summers will talk to the class for about twenty minutes. Mrs Summers works for a charity called Oxfam. She will talk about trying to overcome hunger and poverty in the world. I will be in the classroom during the entire lesson.'

Susan's need for routine and order may cause you to consider how best to make the transition in RE from one topic to another, or from one religion to another. For example, having spent some weeks studying 'Christianity and Islam in the Media', you may plan to change the topic entirely in order to make a study of 'Hinduism and the belief in Reincarnation.' Again, fully briefing Susan about the change, indeed explaining what topics will be studied, when they will be studied and for how long, can be of help to pupils generally. Establishing clear boundaries between topics can also be of help. Making use of the natural breaks around fixed holidays can also be an advantage. However, visual reminders of a topic change, perhaps using colour or a separate display area, will help Susan and young people generally to organise and make sense of the information they are expected to learn.

Some strategies you or the TA could try

Susan may have an ability to recall factual information about religions but may have a weakness when understanding or if abstract thought is required. For example, Susan may know the names and order of all the books in the Bible. However, if asked, 'Why is the Bible called a holy book?' Susan may appear bemused and offer only a literal response, 'Because it's holy.'

It would seem appropriate to tailor Susan's RE so that there is a focus on her strength, the learning of factual information about RE. However, such a programme of work would fall well short of what would normally be regarded as RE. Before deciding how Susan can best be taught RE you should consider if Susan's weakness for understanding is because she has no real awareness of emotions and feelings and it is this which leads her to make only factual or literal responses. Or perhaps it is the fact that Susan shows little emotion or feelings in her own life and this disguises more than might seem to be the case.

'What would you do' activities
Susan might have little or nothing to say if asked, 'Why is the Hajj important to Muslims?' The 'why' suggests an uncovering of the emotions and feelings of others which, expressed in this way, Susan has difficulty responding to. However, you should consider other strategies, which Susan may find less inhibiting. If Susan were asked, 'What would you do?' rather than, 'What are

others feeling?' her response might be a good deal less stunted. For example, Susan might be able to make a much better response to the Hajj task if she were asked, 'You are the manager of a small business. Four Muslims you employ ask for three weeks' leave so that they can go on Hajj. It is a very busy time of the year for your business. What do you do?'

Symbolism and metaphor

Susan may experience difficulty understanding religious metaphor and symbolism, as in statements like, 'Heaven is up there', 'the Bread of Life', 'the Mother of the Book', 'the straight path', ' felt the Holy Spirit' and 'the House of God'. The religious concepts tied up in such statements are notoriously difficult to unravel. Susan may need help over a period of time, in order for her to slowly develop her understanding of this sort of language.

Explicit statements

When exploring the meaning of symbolic religious concepts, a useful strategy may be to invite students to attempt to pair up symbolic religious statements with statements which explicitly deny a literal interpretation. For example, 'Heaven is up there' does not mean 'Heaven is several miles up', and 'The House of God' doesn't mean, 'God is sitting inside the Ka'bah'. People with ASD often need very clear and explicit statements in order for them to understand. However, this does not form the end of the discussion but merely marks the beginning. Being explicit provides the basis on which further class discussion may take place, permitting a more sophisticated understanding to emerge.

Visual support

As is true of many people with ASD, Susan may be a strong visual thinker. Visual images and diagrams can be a valuable strategy for teaching abstract religious concepts. For example, a visual diagram might help Susan understand the Hindu belief that both Rama and Krishna and others are incarnations of the the Hindu god Vishnu.

Examination preparation

If Susan is working towards an exam leading to a national accreditation, careful preparation is needed

- Susan will need to be told as soon as possible the date, time and length of the examination.

- Susan should be given a good idea of how many other people will be in the room or hall taking the exam and who will be adjudicating.

- The seating arrangements and a plan of where she will be sitting may help Susan cope with any sense of anxiety.

- If Susan is hypersensitive to extraneous sounds, like the squeaky shoes of the invigilator or the buzz from fluorescent lights, she may be helped by awareness of relaxation techniques, or more directly, if permitted, by the use of ear plugs.

- It may be advisable for Susan to be allowed to enter early into the space in which the exam will take place as she may need time in order to adjust to the new environment. It is not unknown for students with ASD to have to touch all of the walls of an examination room before they felt sufficiently comfortable to sit the exam.

Appendices

INSET Activity: SEN and Disability Act 2001 (SENDA)

1 The SEN and Disability Act 2001 amends the Disability Discrimination Act 1995 to include schools' and LEAs' responsibility to provide for pupils and students with disabilities.

2 The definition of a disability in this Act is:
'someone who has a physical or mental impairment that has an effect on his or her ability to carry out normal day to day activities. The effect must be:
- substantial (that is more than minor or trivial); and
- long term (that is, has lasted or is likely to last for at least a year or for the rest of the life of the person affected); and
- adverse.'

Activity: List any pupils that you come across that would fall into this category.

3 The act states that the responsible body for a school must take such steps as it is reasonable to take to ensure that disabled pupils and disabled prospective pupils are not placed at substantial disadvantage in comparison with those who are not disabled.

Activity: Give an example of something which might be considered 'a substantial disadvantage'.

4 The duty on the school to make reasonable adjustments is anticipatory. This means that a school should not wait until a disabled pupil seeks admission to consider what adjustments it might make generally to meet the needs of disabled pupils.

Activity: Think of two reasonable adjustments that could be made in your school/department.

5 The school has a duty to plan strategically for increasing access to the school education. This includes provision of information for pupils and parents (e.g. Braille or taped versions of brochures), improving the physical environment for disabled students and increasing access to the curriculum by further differentiation.

Activity: Consider ways of increasing access to the school for a pupil requesting admission who has Down's Syndrome with low levels of literacy and a heart condition that affects strenuous physical activity.

6 Schools need to be proactive in seeking out information about a pupil's disability (by establishing good relationships with parents and carers, asking about disabilities during admission interviews, etc.) and ensuring that all staff who might come across the pupil are aware of the pupil's disability.

Activity: List the opportunities that occur in your school for staff to gain information about disabled students. How can these be improved on?

Reciprocal discussion

A key aspect of religious education is establishing an environment of mutual respect in the classroom where all pupils feel confident to express their opinions and ask questions.

Arranging seats in a circle can help to create an appropriate atmosphere, and displaying the 'turn-taking rules' can help to remind pupils of your expectations.

The use of 'speech cards' can also be effective. Give out two or three cards to each pupil. They have to 'throw in' a card each time they contribute to the discussion. This can help to discourage individuals from 'wasting' their turn (for example by making disparaging remarks); when their cards have been used – they have used up their 'air-time'. This approach also overcomes the problem of one or two pupils dominating the session. (See 'Turn-taking' template on CD)

Nominating a member of the group to listen to the discussion and give feedback at the end of the session can also alert pupils to the fact that what they say is being 'recorded'. Ask for a volunteer to do this, or use it as a way of giving responsibility to a particular individual.

Spelling

A full glossary of key words of six religious traditions, and their meanings, is available from QCA. See Glossary of Terms Order Code RE/94/065 ISBN 1 85838 0413 £4.00 (1994) (QCA website: www.qca.org.uk).

It is important for pupils to build up a working knowledge of key words and technical terms used within each religion, and regular practice of reading and spelling these words will help (little and often). As many different sorts of alphabet are involved, words do not always correspond to our phonetic system and pupils will need to develop visual memory skills to remember words such as Qur'an, Sikh, Kippah, etc. Displaying words around the room will help to reinforce the spelling of key words, and it may be useful to provide pupils with individual lists to keep in their books/folders. Definition lists can be completed for homework .

As well as the words specific to different faith traditions, there are more generic words which may prove difficult for pupils with special needs to learn, and a little time spent on looking closely at these words, sorting out the 'tricky' bits (the *ie* in 'believe', *h* in 'Christ' and 'Christian', *que* in 'Mosque') and practising the spelling can save time in the long term. The '***Look, Say, Cover, Write, Check***' approach uses all the senses and is especially effective when adopted as a whole school approach to spelling. Always encourage pupils to 'have a go' at a word they are unsure about – giving them the right number of letters can help, e.g. if they ask how to spell 'disciple', the teacher/TA might use a scrap of paper to outline the extent of the word.

_ _ _ _ _ _ _ _

then ask, 'What do you think it begins with?' The pupil usually knows this.

d _ _ _ _ _ _ _

build up the word, using what he knows:

d i s _ _ _ l e

fill in the gaps for him, then encourage him to ***look*** at the word, ***say*** it, perhaps trace it in the air, write it – then ***cover*** it up and try to ***write*** it from memory. ***Check*** if it is correct – if not, have another go. This is much more effective than merely telling the pupil how to spell something (which he forgets for next time) or making him do spelling corrections by merely copying from a model.

The writing process

Thinking

- Take some time to think about what to write: what order to do things in (make a plan or mind-map; beginning–middle–end; paragraph headings; subtitles). Make sure you are doing what you have been asked to do.

- Prepare by talking things through (planning on paper if it is complicated).

- Find out what you need to know (make up some questions you need to answer; look in books, in your own notes or on the internet; ask other people; make observations).

First draft

In jotter or on rough paper.

Revising

Writing often needs redrafting. The changes you make will result in your work becoming more clear, more interesting, more concise or more powerful. Ask yourself:

- Are things in the right order?

- Do all the sentences mean what I want them to mean?

- Does every word count? Can anything be cut out?

- Are the words well chosen? Can I think of any which are more interesting, more accurate or more unusual?

- Have I repeated the same word, or said the same thing twice, without meaning to?

- Is it legible?

- Is it interesting?

- Is it accurate?

- Have I checked spelling and punctuation?

It is always better to revise your work after a break. Come back to it the next day if possible – you will see it with new eyes and find it easier to make a good assessment. Get someone else to read it and say what they think (if you're brave enough) – or read it aloud to them.

Writing frame: Muslims

The main beliefs Muslims have about God are that . . .

Muslims also believe that God is . . .

Christians and Muslims have similar views about God, as in both religions they believe . . .

However, Muslims do not believe . . .

My own view about God is that . . .

Starter activities

Starter activities should capture children and get lessons off to a snappy start. They might be used to remind and reinforce the previous lesson or set up the theme of the forthcoming lesson.

Quiz question

Working in groups of four, each group is asked to come up with five questions and their answers on a particular theme, e.g. five questions about: the fast of Ramadan, how Easter is celebrated, the Jewish Sabbath, the Gurdwara, the story of Rama and Sita, Holy Communion.

What would be missed?

Working in pairs, ask the pupils, 'What would be missed?' if a particular religious ritual or ceremony was not undertaken, e.g. What would be missed if . . . Muslims never went on pilgrimage? Buddhists didn't meditate? a Christian never prayed? the Bible didn't exist? Sikhs didn't wear the five Ks? Christmas wasn't celebrated?

Who am I?

Ask for a volunteer. Attach a label to the volunteer's head on which is written the name of a person whose life or achievements will be explored in the RE lesson. For example, Moses, Desmond Tutu, Muhammad, Mother Teresa, the Buddha, Guru Nanak. The volunteer may ask 20 questions, to which the rest of the class may only answer 'yes' or 'no'. The object of the game is to guess the name on the label before the volunteer runs out of questions.

Snowball

Recall what you can remember learning about in the last RE lesson. Share your ideas with a partner to produce a more accurate account. Share your ideas now in a group of four to produce the most accurate account you can remember. Share your account with the rest of the class.

A useful model lesson structure

PRESENT the religion being learned

If a particular religion features in the lesson ensure that pupils are clear what religion it is. Make use of a starter, which captures the pupils in the first few minutes of the lesson. Share with the pupils the aims of the lesson. Give children with learning difficulties, or pupils that have a sensory impairment, a copy of any relevant text so that, perhaps with the help of the teaching assistant, they are not slowed down or involved in unproductive copying.

ACTIVE learning strategies

Plan a series of short, varied activities which breaks the lesson up so that the interest of the pupils is retained. Avoid passive activities, like teacher talk or reading. Instead plan more memorable activities which require the pupils to be involved and to do things like act out, speak, report back or move about the classroom. Identify pupils that may not be fully engaged and attempt to involve them so that individuals are not sidelined or feeling left out.

LEARN from religion

Build in thinking or reflecting time into most lessons. Identify, or encourage the pupils to identify, what is of value or relevance they can learn from the material being studied. Build in thinking or reflecting time into most lessons so that pupils have an opportunity to consider their own position, or judgement, or perhaps consider what, if anything, they can take away from the lesson which may have application, or offer insights into their own life.

DEEPEN and probe

Reinforce and summarise what has been gained from the lesson. Extend and attempt to deepen all of the pupils' thinking and ideas with more probing questions. Encourage pupils to think about their thinking. How well have they presented their ideas, their arguments or reasons? Are there consequences, evidence or scenarios which they have not considered? Is their thinking consistent? Is their reasoning well supported and persuasive? Is there additional evidence to support what they have been saying?

PLENARY and feedback

Allocate plenty of time for the plenary so that it is not rushed at the end. Avoid taking over the plenary and using it as an opportunity for the teacher to tell the children what the teacher believes they have learnt from the lesson. Encourage the pupils to talk about what they learnt or gained from the lesson. Use the plenary as an assessment opportunity to judge how well pupils have understood, what might have to be revisited or better explained, which pupils might need particular support and how to best guide pupils, or structure the scheme of work in the future, in order to best support learning.

Guidance for teaching assistants

Golden rules

- Avoid providing answers but allow pupils to think for themselves.

- In RE different views are permitted but disrespectful language is not.

- Avoid too much focus on the who, what and where but instead encourage exploration of the why, the meaning and the significance.

- Avoid giving the impression that world religions are weird, odd or that their primary interest is as an exotic novelty.

Personal information

- In RE you will learn a lot about pupils' beliefs, values, concerns and attitudes.

- Build on and respect personal information and experience.

- RE is very person-centred. Listen to what young people have to say and build a relationship with each child.

- Beware of differences in culture. Use examples which are relevant to the child you are working with. Not all pupils identify with TV soaps, football, pop music and celebrity.

Encourage pupils to participate in class but be aware of individual differences

- Don't just talk; draw, mime, use analogies and examples, and give children quiet thinking time.

- Encourage learning through active strategies like acting out, demonstrating, reporting back and explaining.

- Try to get each pupil to participate in extended speaking by avoiding questions which require little more than one-word answers. Pose problems which require answers of more length.

- Ensure that the most vocal children do not dominate the lessons. Encourage the quiet or shy (or perhaps the more reflective) pupil to participate and share their views.

- Don't assume that students that are members of a particular religion necessarily always provide the most informed, accurate or wisest insights into that religion.

Relationships between teachers and TAs: Issues for discussion

- What will you expect from the Assistant?

- Do all of the RE staff have a clear understanding of the roles and responsibilities of the TA?

- What can they reasonably ask a TA to do?

- Will he/she be expected to work with groups or individuals?

- What will be the status of the Teaching Assistant?

- How are Teaching Assistants referred to?

- Are pupils expected to treat them with the same degree of respect as they would a teacher?

- Should they suggest and make additional materials?

- Do you want them to write in pupils' books? If so, should it be in a different colour?

- Are TAs responsible for care needs?

- Will the TA be involved in planning?

- How will he/she feed back information about pupils' progress?

- Does he/she understand the importance of confidentiality?

- Will there be regular meetings between the HoD and TA?

- Will they be expected to attend staff meetings?

- Should they provide written notes which could be incorporated into an IEP?

- Are TAs responsible for setting up computers and finding other specialist equipment?

- Will opportunities be provided for him/her to become familiar with the hardware, software and teaching needs?

- Will training be available?

- Will support materials be provided?

> ## Does prayer work?

Does prayer work?

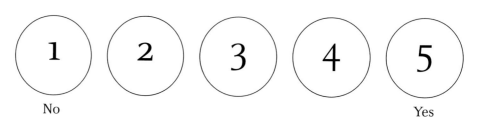

No   Yes

On a scale of 1 to 5 choose the number you most agree with.

Write your number onto a piece of paper (don't sign it).

Put your paper into a box.

Pass the box around and remove one piece of paper.

Place on the floor the numbers 1 to 5.

Everyone that has a paper with 1 on it, form a line by the number 1 on the floor.

Do the same for the other four numbers until the class has formed a human bar chart of their view about prayer.

Community of enquiry

Think about the picture quietly.

What question does it raise for you?

My question is . . .

Share your question with a partner and then with two others.

Decide which question you like most.

Our question is . . .

Cut out the question you like most and fix it to the display board.

The Crucifixion: Two views

Look at two different depictions of the crucifixion, e.g. Matthias Grunewald (dark, sombre, tragic) and Sanzio Raphael (victorious, serene, uplifting).

Work with a partner. Suggest how artists may have different views about the crucifixion.

In a group of four share your ideas.

As a group of four agree what the two artists' views might be.

Which view comes closest to your own opinion? Give your reasons.

Share your ideas with the rest of the class.

The Good Samaritan

The Good Samaritan is a famous story Jesus told.
Luke chapter 10

What do you think the story tells us?

How might a person be a Good Samaritan today?

I think the story of the Good Samaritan tells us . . .

An example of how a young person might be a Good Samaritan today might be . . .

Pyramid activity: What prayer?

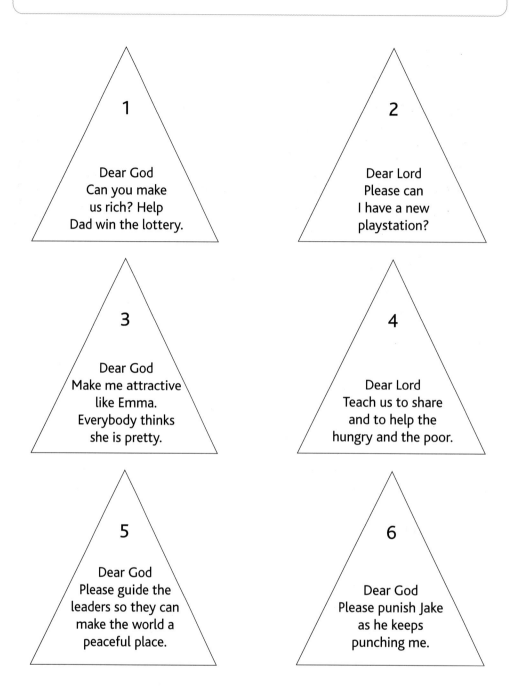

1

Dear God
Can you make
us rich? Help
Dad win the lottery.

2

Dear Lord
Please can
I have a new
playstation?

3

Dear God
Make me attractive
like Emma.
Everybody thinks
she is pretty.

4

Dear Lord
Teach us to share
and to help the
hungry and the poor.

5

Dear God
Please guide the
leaders so they can
make the world a
peaceful place.

6

Dear God
Please punish Jake
as he keeps
punching me.

- Cut out the six triangles.
- Arrange the triangles into a pyramid.
- Place the comment you agree with most at the top.
- Place the three you like least at the base of the pyramid.
- Place the two comments which you quite agree with in the middle.
- Give a reason for your answer.

Useful contacts

http://re-xs.ucsm.ac.uk	information on different faiths, glossary, images, etc.
www.reonline.org.uk	virtual tours, festivals, school websites
www.religiousresources.org	directory of internet resources
www.hindukids.org	animated stories (with audio) – great fun for pupils

Association for Religious Education Inspectors, Advisers and Consultants (AREIAC). The professional association for Religious Education inspectors, advisers and consultants. It has published guidance on inspection issues in RE and (with NASACRE) a guide to Agreed Syllabuses in England and Wales. AREIAC liaises with the Department for Education and Skills (DfES), QCA and the Teacher Training Agency (TTA) on RE-related issues.
www.areiac.org.uk

Professional Council for Religious Education (PcfRE). The subject teacher association for RE professionals in primary and secondary schools and higher education, providing representation, publications and courses to promote professional development.
www.pcfre.org.uk

TheREsite. TheREsite is at the centre of a family of sites which includes The RE Directory, REfuel and Places of Worship, providing links to resources and information.
www.theresite.org.uk

References

DfES (2001) *Revised Special Educational Needs Code of Practice.* London: DfES.

DfES (2004) *Removing Barriers to Achievement: The Government's Strategy for SEN.* London: HMSO.

DfES/QCA (2004) *The Non-Statutory National Framework for Religious Education,* QCA/04/1336. London: QCA.

Hammond, J., Hay, D., Moxon, J. *et al.* (1990) *New Methods in RE Today.* Harlow: Oliver & Boyd.

Ofsted Subject Reports 2002/03: *Religious Education in Secondary Schools.* HMI 1989. February.

www.ofsted.gov.uk/publications/

Ofsted (2003) *Special Educational Needs in the Mainstream.* London: Ofsted.

QCA (2000) *Religious Education: Non-Statutory Guidance,* QCA/00/576. London: QCA.

QCA (2001) *Religious Education: Planning, Teaching and Assessing the Curriculum for Pupils with Learning Difficulties,* QCA/01/750. Sudbury: QCA.

Stakes, R. and Hornby, G. (2000) *Meeting Special Needs in Mainstream Schools: A Practical Guide for Teachers.* London: David Fulton Publishers.

Booth, T., Ainscow, M., Black-Hawkins, K., Vaughan, M. and Shaw, L. (2000) *Index for Inclusion.* Bristol: CSIE.